"The wisdom of years observing, listening, and engaging in debate and reflection become distilled into why changing church is needed and how it can happen. In two dioceses I have seen the deep value of this work. Read it and be blessed."

— PAUL BUTLER, Bishop of Durham

"This book and its authors offer a wealth of wisdom and experience on what it takes to make a church, a community, and a denomination work. They highlight the intense hard work of cultivating and maintaining a community but show that true change comes from action-focused transformation. In formulating where we want our churches and our world to go, we must first reconsider the ways in which our communities need to reflect our truest beliefs and how to act on them. Wes Granberg-Michaelson and Pat Keifert offer a series of challenges that are at once inspiring, practical, provocative, actionable, and hopeful. This is a handbook for what is called the 'missional church.' It is a key resource for those pondering how they might actually put faith into action and contribute to communities that are radically transforming the world."

— JIM WALLIS, Sojourners

"While many of those who participate in North American churches agree that change is a necessary component of a vital and viable future, they are also perplexed with respect to identifying and bringing about the changes that are needed. In this very readable volume, two highly respected and seasoned leaders distill their years of wisdom in helping churches fruitfully navigate the challenges of change. An ideal volume for congregations seeking practical help in the quest for a more faithful and vibrant witness."

— JOHN R. FRANKE,
Gospel and Our Culture Network

"Keifert and Granberg-Michaelson channel a wealth of practical experience into guiding denominational and congregational change. Their recommendations offer deep wisdom to churches seeking missional transformation. In short, this book rings true. I recommend it very highly for pastors, denominational leaders, and church folks who seek guidance in this missional age."

— DANA L. ROBERT,
Boston University School of Theology

"Drawing on more than four decades of work with congregations, denominations, and other expressions of the church across the world, Pat Keifert and Wes Granberg-Michaelson have provided a profoundly helpful handbook for church leaders of all sorts and settings. This book is focused on discernment over strategic plans, reaches beyond programs and techniques to address the deep culture of communities, is rooted in communal and public spiritual practices, and is eminently practical. It really ought to be in the hands of every leader who knows that the transformation of the church is a life-or-death matter but isn't quite sure how to open the communities they serve to the transforming power of the Holy Spirit."

— BISHOP WILLIAM GAFKJEN,
Indiana-Kentucky Synod, ELCA

"This book is full of hard-won wisdom from two leaders who have spent decades successfully leading change in the church. Their core learnings are distilled here in an accessible, practical form—learnings that explain why so many change efforts fail. This is a profoundly hopeful book, grounded in God's mission and drawing on the best organizational thinking."

— DWIGHT ZSCHEILE,
Luther Seminary

"A prophetic call to reconsider processes of congregational and denominational transformation, rooted in cultural change, discernment, and creative, non-anxious leadership. Keifert and Granberg-Michaelson provide not only a convincing account of the life-or-death issues facing churches but also clear, accessible, simple practices and ways of being that address such issues. Their approach promises a deeper participation in God's missional activity among the people of God and thus a reclaiming of those purposes which are at the heart of the church's vocation. A wonderfully engaging, timely, and hopeful book."

— MIKE HARRISON,
Bishop of Dunwich

"This isn't just a book for churches in the USA! As someone who has been working with the theology and practices outlined in this book for nearly ten years in the UK, I can testify to the veracity of the authors' claims about how churches change. I have watched it happen, without any sense of a 'magic formula' being applied, just the hard work of discerning what God is up to and joining in. This is also a book for denominational leaders as we hear how the systems that support local churches can also change—down to their very foundations. In fact, this book is highly applicable all over the world where churches face a changed world around them and have to find a godly way to respond. Read it, act on it, and be changed."

— REV. CANON DR. NIGEL ROOMS,
Church Mission Society

How Change Comes to Your Church

A Guidebook for Church Innovations

Patrick Keifert
and
Wesley Granberg-Michaelson

WILLIAM B. EERDMANS PUBLISHING COMPANY
GRAND RAPIDS, MICHIGAN

Wm. B. Eerdmans Publishing Co.
4035 Park East Court SE, Grand Rapids, Michigan 49546
www.eerdmans.com

Published 2019
Printed in the United States of America

25 24 23 22 21 20 19   1 2 3 4 5 6 7

ISBN 978-0-8028-7624-9

Library of Congress Cataloging-in-Publication Data

Names: Keifert, Patrick R., 1950- author.
Title: How change comes to your church : a guidebook for church
    innovations / Patrick Keifert and Wesley Granberg-Michaelson.
Description: Grand Rapids : William B. Eerdmans Publishing
    Company, 2019. | Includes bibliographical references. |
    Summary: "The authors identify key elements that are a
    necessary part of change within congregations and focus on the
    necessary alterations in church culture and innovative spiritual
    practices that establish the foundation for durable, missional
    change"—Provided by publisher.
Identifiers: LCCN 2019022636 | ISBN 9780802876249 (trade
    paperback)
Subjects: LCSH: Church renewal. | Change—Religious
    aspects—Christianity.
Classification: LCC BV600.3 .K45 2019 | DDC 262.001/7—dc23
LC record available at https://lccn.loc.gov/2019022636

Contents

Gift. Kenny Bluese. 4/24/2023

Contents

Introduction

Starting Up Close—a Congregational Story

Helen Booker is the president of Christ Church in a town of two thousand inhabitants. A nearly lifetime member of this congregation, she has recently retired from administrative leadership in the local school district and brings tremendous energy, life experience, and a deep abiding faith in Christ and his church, including her local Christ Church. She also joins a certain impatience to a practical willingness to work with people where they are in their lives.

Her impatience grows out of a sense that Christ Church continues to atrophy, not only in numbers—in terms of both attendance and finances—but also in excitement and energy for mission and ministry. As a school administrator, she knows the community has a growing younger population, since the schools are stretching to serve a wider range of cultures, economic classes, and family patterns in her community. She sees the habits and physical space of Christ Church reinforcing the patterns of ministry developed over a century as an immigrant church, habits and physical space that no longer foster a lively, growing, Christian church in her rural community.

She has worked with other rural schools in settings in which population patterns are increasingly challenging for all civic and church organizations because young people leave and never return. In these communities, the median age of the inhabitants is rising, and real numbers are decreasing. The consolidation of schools has increasingly been the answer. The same pressure to consolidate churches in these areas has come from denominational executives and some members of local churches. Often, in strong reaction to denominational pressure to consolidate services, rural churches have refused to join reorganizational patterns "from above." In several communities, this dynamic has led to an increasing number of congregations as local churches have splintered in struggles over survival and differences over various moral and cultural issues.

However, in the community surrounding Christ Church, median age is going down, and new people are moving to the area. New people have little or no ties to the church, let alone ties to the immigrant culture that founded Christ Church. Further, Christ Church is in a community that has attracted an upper-middle-class retirement center, which brings significant jobs as well as residents to this rural town.

Because of this, Helen saw tremendous need and opportunity for Christ Church. She was frustrated by the clear failure of Christ Church to reach out to form community with either the new younger persons or the new emerging retirement community. She was also aware of and sympathetic to denominational officials who wanted Christ Church to extend resources to the struggling rural churches in the surrounding communities. Hence her frustration and impatience.

Helen shared her perception of the lack of connection between the emerging town and the existing Christ Church with her pastor, Chris. Chris was impressed with Helen's insights into the emerging community and with her clear sense of frustration and impatience. Chris saw in Helen an ideal leader for church development in Christ Church. Chris had learned in her previous ministry experience how vital lay leaders are to sustained growth in the local church.

Chris is an experienced pastor and leader. She served in the US Air Force after college as an officer and then felt the call to ministry. Initially, she served on a large church staff of a Midwestern suburban church of her denomination. After seven years in that call, she accepted a call as a church developer. She took the courses offered by her denomination on new-church development, drawing together her strong administrative experience in the military with her considerable interpersonal skills.

She started a new church development in a suburban setting in the Midwest that initially went very well. In the first three years, worship attendance grew each year simply through Chris visiting the new families who were moving to the growing suburb. She developed a core congregation, what she called her "church family," who gave generous financial support to the new church start. Since most of them were two-career couples, with very young families, they had less time and more money to contribute to the growing congregation. They were attracted to Chris, and they were completely committed to her leadership. As a result, by the end of year four, the new church required no further financial support from the denomination. Everything seemed well for a bright future.

Over the next ten years, even though the congregation continued to incorporate new members each year, worship attendance and other indicators of church participation remained level. As the "church family" went through life changes, they tended to move out of active participation, while Chris would bring into the "church family" newly arrived members. The actual numbers and active membership remained relatively constant. After fifteen years, she was convinced that it was time to move on and to allow a new clergy leader to take the congregation to its next stage of growth. Chris then took a call to Christ Church.

Chris took the call to Christ Church believing, as Helen did, that the potential for a vital and flourishing future was clearly present. During the next ten years, however, the same pattern developed in Christ Church that had developed in the new church start. Chris continued to visit new people in the community, bring them into the church family, but seemed to lose as many out the back door as she brought into the front door.

She became even more disturbed when she learned that her previous congregation had called a new pastor who lasted only three years and left the congregation in deep conflict, with less than half the worship attendance there had been when Chris left. In conversations with that pastor, who called himself the "unintentional interim pastor," she learned how her "church family" found his person and leadership style in such a stark contrast to hers that they became embroiled in one conflict after another. Each conflict, some over significant issues and others over seemingly insignificant matters, drained the vitality of the congregation. The congregation was considering closing.

Chris became convinced that some of the patterns in both churches reflected her failure to develop lay leadership that owned a sense of vision for the congregation and a sense that that vision was theirs to achieve. Chris felt sure that she needed to find a different model of lay leadership development in order to create a sustainable, vital church. So when Helen presented herself, with her capacities as an experienced community leader, her devotion as a faithful Christian, and her sense of wanting more for Christ Church, Chris saw a chance to develop a lay leadership around Helen more focused on the future vitality of Christ Church.

Chris knew that her role as pastor needed to change significantly, but she was not sure how to navigate the change. She was filled with a sense that this was a moment of life or death for Christ Church, but she was wise enough to know that she did not even understand the actual challenge facing her. She knew that her community was not filled with persons with any church ties. Indeed, most of the new persons in the community did not even have parents who were members of a church. The church was not even on their radar screen. She also knew that the faithful were mostly content with their situation, happy to continue the slow but certain demise of Christ Church.

Chris and Helen saw each other as sharing a sense of possibility and an equally great sense of disease and frankly incompetence to know how to move forward. They decided to hire an outside church consulting firm that did stewardship programs for churches. This appealed to key new members who had experienced effective fundraising programs led by this consulting group in other churches. Indeed, a handful of them volunteered to pay for the consultants. So they proceeded.

The consulting group brought a state-of-the-art process for congregational fundraising to Christ Church. The initial year-long process developed seemingly strong energy for raising money for a new church building on a site more suitable to the emerging community. A new site was purchased by a handful of the congregation in anticipation of this new church building. Then the reality of the existing congregation's attitudes and beliefs came to the fore. They reacted strongly against this new building project, and the forward momentum ended.

While the challenges facing Helen and Chris have dynamics peculiar to their setting, the underlying patterns in their situation, emerging over the past thirty or so years, are typical across a far wider scope of the church in the USA. Further, often in startling ways, the challenges of churches in rural America are similar to those of churches in urban settings.

The Wider Congregational Picture

The United States is home to an estimated 350,000 church congregations. These churches provide a local place for worship, community, and witness for those who identify as Christians. But experts project that between 30 to 40 percent of these churches—that is, at least 100,000—are likely to close in the next thirty years.

The average size of a US congregation is 186 people. But that figure is misleading. If you examine the median size, meaning the point at which an equal number of congregations are larger and smaller, you'll see that it is just seventy-five. (This metric measures those who regularly attend Sunday worship.) About half of all congregations in the US are small churches, yet they comprise only 11 percent of all those people attending church. On the other hand, congregations with 350 or more members, which make up only 10 percent of all congregations, are filled with 50 percent of those typically attending church on Sunday.

Over half of all Protestant congregations—including mainline and evangelical—sense that they need to change, and they are worried. The Hartford Institute for Religion Research completed a comprehensive study of US congregations in 2015. It included questions about congregational change. Twenty-one percent agreed with the statement "We need to change to increase our vitality and viability, but the congregation does not seem to realize it and/or doesn't want to make the necessary changes." And 32 percent said, "We are slowly changing, but not fast enough or significantly enough."

When broken down by congregational size, the results were more revealing. Seventy-four percent of those congregations with fewer than 50 people agreed that needed changes were happening either too slowly or not at all. Sixty percent of congregations with between 50 and 100 people agreed, but in congregations of 100 to 250, only 32 percent had that belief. In congregations of 250 or greater, 37 percent saw the need for change that was not being recognized or addressed sufficiently.

Congregations able to make changes are more likely to experience higher vitality. The Hartford survey of US congregations included a series of questions asking them to assess their own vitality, spiritually and organizationally, and then the survey related this to a congregation's ability to embrace change. Of those most positive about their proven capacity to continually change, adapt, and improve, 62 percent reported having high congregational vitality. In contrast, only 11 percent of those congregations not able to recognize or sufficiently embrace change described themselves as having high vitality.

What, then, do congregations perceive as the barriers to change? Here again, evidence from the Hartford study, as well as from other sources, is revealing. One-third of congregations cite the "lack of unifying and energizing vision or direction." That figure rises to 40 percent among congregations of 250 or more in attendance. Another 30 percent of congregations say they lack "workable, concrete models that provide realistic but vitalizing alternatives to the status quo." The other most frequently cited barrier was insufficient resources of money and energy—a barrier highlighted strongly by smaller congregations.

So, the picture that emerges is a startling one. Most congregations in the US recognize their need for change. Further, it's clear this is linked to their ability to become or remain vital, both spiritually and organizationally. Additionally, they have a sense of what they need, and the barriers to such change.

But they don't know how to change.

Denominational Structures

Most of these congregations belong to wider institutional bodies, usually called denominations. Some have other looser forms of affiliation, and about 10 percent of congregations are independent of any wider denominational or organizational belonging. Denominational structures typically function at several levels, beginning with local organizational bodies normally grouping twenty-five to fifty congregations together, then moving to regional structures, and finally to national and, in some cases, international bodies. Depending on the denomination's understanding of authority in the church, these various structures carry different levels of responsibility in the governance of the denomination and its congregations and carry out a variety of programs for ministry, mission, education, and pastoral support.

Today, denominational bodies at all levels generally reflect the institutional anxiety of their congregations. At the simplest, superficial level, they see their overall number of members and finances decreasing. With a small number of exceptions, and cutting across theological differences, denominations have fewer congregations, fewer members, and fewer dollars than a decade ago. That diminishment creates perpetual efforts to reduce, restructure, and refocus the institutional expressions of denominations.

Those in positions of denominational leadership, in most cases, are clear about the need for some kind of change. But beyond mere institutional survival, the fundamental, driving purposes for change are often un-articulated, which means they are not well understood. Moreover, the methods and practices which can engender foundational change seem elusive. Like their congregations, the bishops, stated clerks, general secretaries, presidents, district superintendents, regional synod executives, overseers, general ministers, and others leading denominational structures are often uncertain about the most promising pathways that might actually produce the lasting changes they desire.

The story of one such fictional leader from a fictional denomination, created from the facts and real stories of those daily engaged in this call to ministry, should be illustrative.

A Denomination's Story of Attempting Change

The Reverend Sheldon Keating pored over the latest update of his denomination's annual membership report despondently. His vice president for research, records, and archives had just brought it to his office that morning. "It's not good news, Sheldon," he announced. "I really thought the first signs of the TMM plan would begin to show up by now in the numbers. But the demographic headwinds are stronger than we anticipated."

Three years earlier, at age forty-three, Reverend Keating had become the new president and executive minister of his denomination, the Christian Evangelical Alliance of North America. He had left a brief but successful career in advertising to go into the ministry when he was thirty, and launched his church plant in Denver before even graduating from seminary. His entrepreneurial, charismatic style appealed to younger families and fueled new growth in the southeast area of greater Denver. In only seven years, the church had gained a thousand members, and then satellite campuses had sprung up, the most recent one just north of Colorado Springs. Pushing close to three thousand members in only thirteen years, Community of Life was a denominational success story.

The Christian Evangelical Alliance (CEA) has its roots in Scandinavian immigration to the United States in the late nineteenth century. Impacted by the Pietistic revivals in Europe, immigrants desired freedom from their state churches, and once they moved to the US, their new denomination blossomed, particularly throughout the upper Midwest and then beyond. Now with about two thousand largely white congregations, it has three affiliated colleges and two seminaries. In the 1950s its denominational structures grew with its congregations, organized into these areas: World Mission, Christian Education, Ministry Preparation, Word and Life Publishing, New Church Development, Racial Ministries (an ongoing fight has still not resulted in changing the name first given in 1962), Domestic Mission (which is perpetually trying to redefine its present mandate), and Retirement Benefits. Each has separate boards, directors, and segregated budgets.

The Office of the President and Executive Minister includes the research, records, and archives vice president, one secretary and part-time administrative help from a librarian staff member at one of the seminaries, plus a special assistant to the president, whose varied responsibilities are supposed to include working with the president on matters of social witness and church unity. The president also has an events coordinator, whose primary task is to guide preparations for the denomination's Annual Assembly, held each summer at Crusader College (a five-year commission could still not agree on a recommendation to change its name) outside Oshkosh, Wisconsin.

But despite ambitious new church plants begun in the 1960s and sporadic financial boosts from denominational fund drives—the most recent, "Harvest Wind," was completed three years ago—the CEA had been slowly but consistently losing members in the last fifty years. The average church size when Keating became president was fifty-eight. Statistics, dutifully collected, showed decreases in baptisms, Sunday school attendance, offerings, and worship attendance. A significant number of congregations established prior to World War II, mostly in Midwestern rural areas, were hovering around fifty faithful members, in small communities that never recovered from the 2008 recession.

Of course, there were bright spots, and these were showcased at every Annual Assembly. An Asian pastor of a new CEA church plant in Portland, Latino pastors of new churches in Chicago, and Somali pastors of a couple of new churches in the Twin Cities were heralded as proof of the CEA's bright future. When the Reverend Sheldon Keating was invited as a keynote speaker to the Annual Assembly, he suddenly emerged on the radar of the search committee as a candidate for the CEA's presidency.

The argument for his nomination seemed compelling, fitting the populist mood in the country at large. Reverend Keating had never been part of the denomination's governing structure or offices—in fact, he humorously credited this as one of the obvious reasons for his success in ministry. He often boasted about the latest invitation to serve on a denominational committee or task force that he had just rejected. "I'd rather just do ministry than sit in a stuffy room in Milwaukee moaning about what can't be done in the CEA."

But the search committee chair, Bill Rasmussen, CEO of a large health-care system, was looking for someone to break the CEA out of its bureaucratic lethargy and organizational dysfunction. With a sharp critique of the top three candidates who had emerged on the search committee's list, he convinced the group that they should aggressively pursue Reverend Keating, who was not even a candidate. Rasmussen flew to Denver, took the Reverend and his wife, Katie, out to dinner, and made his case. "Don't you think God could be preparing you as the leader who can demonstrate how to turn around America's fledgling denominations? Don't rest with Community of Life's success. Ask what new horizon is being revealed for your ministry."

Reverend Keating was captivated. He had known he didn't want to stay at Community of Life for his entire ministerial career but didn't really have an exit plan. Katie was reluctant to move back to Milwaukee, but one of their two children had already left for college, and the second was just a year away. It took only a week to make the decision but three months to figure out a process of departure from his congregation, suddenly sent into shock. By the next Annual Assembly, the Reverend Sheldon Keating was installed as the CEA's new president and executive minister.

He came with a plan. And the delegates, especially the lay leaders, loved this fresh, younger, successful leader who could bring new vitality and energy to their denomination. Reverend Keating proposed a program titled "Thriving in Ministry and Mission." It had three parts: (1) Plant two hundred new churches each year, 10 percent of the denomination's current total; (2) Reorganize all the separate boards, agencies, and budgets into one streamlined structure of governance in order to prioritize the CEA's resources; and (3) Ask every congregation to take part in a new "Evangelize Your Neighbor" program, utilizing the best models, such as Alpha. (Its Twitter handle, @AlphaUSA, was emblazoned on a new CEA keychain given to each delegate.)

Reverend Keating left the Annual Assembly dramatically, flying directly to Cleveland to begin a barnstorming tour meeting with each of the CEA's seventeen districts. His plan was to gather as many pastors as possible and introduce himself in "spiritual town halls," set up as

Q&A sessions so the new president could get to know and be known by all the CEA churches. Meanwhile, the assembly had approved his "Commission on Integrated Mission" (CIM) proposal to design a new organizational structure for the CEA. The assembly had also "requested" its seminaries to establish training modules for church planters that could function independently of their MDiv programs.

Problems first surfaced during Reverend Keating's seventeen "spiritual town halls." These Q&A sessions almost always began with a sharp question about the CEA's posture toward homosexuality. While the denomination generally held a conservative position, that was being tested. Most notably, a new, noteworthy CEA church plant in downtown Seattle had begun to thrive, and its program of outreach, with its slogan "Here's a Home for Your Heart," welcomed gay and lesbian persons. Worried conservative members on the CEA's New Church Development Board successfully pressed to cut funds being given to this church plant from the "Harvest Wind" fund drive.

The case quickly became a flash point in the CEA, particularly as it garnered local and then even national press attention. The CEA's traditional stance disapproving of same-sex relationships wasn't constitutionally stipulated and therefore couldn't be uniformly enforced within its polity. The controversy grew, pitting older conservatives and several of its nonwhite pastors against those arguing that congregational autonomy and ministry flexibility were being threatened. Younger CEA pastors pressed Reverend Keating, asking how the CEA could pull the rug out from a promising new church plant while calling for the most ambitious new-church start goals in the CEA's history.

Reverend Keating's Community of Life megachurch had basically followed a "don't ask, don't tell" policy. Two members of its leadership team, including its gifted music and arts coordinator, had separately told the Reverend they were gay, and he simply affirmed them but thanked them profusely for their ongoing discretion. Now as CEA president, Reverend Keating basically didn't want to be bothered with the broader church's controversy over same-sex relationships. He had started calling it the CEA's "most tempting anti-missional distraction." But that didn't fly.

Further, the CEA's conservative establishment saw their institutional power threatened by Reverend Keating's proposed organizational restructuring being developed by the Commission on Integrated Mission (CIM). Resisting it directly would be politically unwise, but they could undermine Reverend Keating's leadership by questioning his reluctance to "draw a clear theological line in society's shifting sands" against same-sex relationships. Restructuring should be delayed, they began to argue, until the CEA could articulate what it believed.

The crucial political move that threw sand in the gears of Reverend Keating's restructuring proposals, however, came from Rev. Dr. Marcus "Doc" Jackson, an outspoken African American CEA pastor in Milwaukee. Jackson had long been a fixture at CEA assemblies, most recently making an impassioned plea for a resolution to support the Black Lives Matter movement; a compromise version died in committee when he withdrew his support.

As chair of the Racial Ministries Board, with effective control of its budget, Jackson attacked the CIM process during his board's report to the assembly. "This so-called streamlined organizational proposal aims to reestablish the old CEA institutional plantation, taking away the voice of African Americans and putting them back into their place. And then the new masters of the CEA will have the power to require servitude to the culture's captivity to same-sex marriage." Conservatives sat back silently, loving every word, and CEA progressives wouldn't publicly criticize anything "Doc" Jackson said.

Reverend Keating's "Evangelize Your Neighbor" initiative also had a hard time gaining traction at the CEA's congregational grass roots. No one, of course, opposed evangelism. But the Reverend had been enamored with Alpha ever since traveling to England when he was still an advertising executive and spending time with Nicky Gumbel at Holy Trinity Brompton, who had become its leader. Further, Reverend Keating assumed that if he as CEA president strongly recommended something, 90 percent of congregations would follow suit.

At a district "spiritual town hall" held in Eagle River in northern Wisconsin, the Reverend Bert Swenson, a revered long-time CEA pastor who had authored a popular short book, *Small Congregations Can Be Beautiful*, zeroed in on Reverend Keating's approach. "Your Alpha courses, with their fancy dinners and slick videos, may work for congregations with young families living in half-a-million-dollar homes in Barrington, Illinois," Swenson began. "But up here in Vilas County, the wise farmers and snowmobile dealers who keep our small churches alive view this as one more example of cultural elites foisting their impractical ideas on places and people they don't respect. Only now, this isn't coming from Washington bureaucrats; it's coming from the CEA's headquarters on Plankington Avenue in Milwaukee."

Swenson's son-in-law was at the "spiritual town hall" and recorded this speech on his iPhone. Once on You-Tube, it began to spread through Swenson's network—his book had been one of the best sellers recently put out by Word and Life Publishing. From there it began to go viral within the CEA, known popularly as the "Watch Bert Take Down Sheldon" video. Pastors skeptical about a denominational evangelism program now had a reason to not cooperate with it without seeming to be against evangelism.

Faculty of the CEA's two seminaries were aghast when they heard of Reverend Keating's proposal for developing a track for training new-church development pastors that could bypass the MDiv requirement. Their normal aversion to institutional change went into overdrive, and the recommendations sent by the assembly to "vigorously pursue these options" got entangled in the seminaries' cumbersome decision-making labyrinths. Reverend Keating was partially successful in getting around this by pushing an existing provision for districts to grant "provisional ministerial authority" to lay pastors and others coming from outside the CEA's formal pastoral pipeline.

Although the number of new-church development pastors coming into the CEA gradually increased, the numerical goals of "Thriving in Ministry and Mission" proved completely unrealistic. Even Reverend Keating's friends began to say, "Planting two hundred new churches in the CEA requires different gifts than starting one megachurch in Denver." And apart from saving the CEA, Reverend Keating's aggressive new-church development plans lacked a compelling, motivating narrative.

Meanwhile, 55 percent of the CEA's congregations were under one hundred members, and those approaching fifty or less were preoccupied with the struggle of survival. Many quietly closed, nearly equaling the number of congregational new starts. In his first three years as president, Keating could point to nearly two hundred newly emerging CEA congregations—an increase from the past, but only one-third of his goal. Further, not all of them survived, and membership in the majority of the CEA's existing congregations continued to decline, as deaths still exceeded baptisms.

Therefore, the numbers in the CEA's annual membership report, which would be distributed at the forthcoming Annual Assembly, were depressing. The downward trend was continuing after three years of effort, visiting every corner of the CEA, meeting with every board and agency, and adding 100,000 miles each year to Reverend Keating's United Airlines mileage account. He looked in vain for any numerical bright spots that he could highlight in his forthcoming presidential report to the assembly. The Reverend wondered what he had done wrong, and even why he had moved to Milwaukee.

Changing the Way Churches Change

Meaningful change in the life of the church, whether at the congregational or the denominational level, is arduous and frequently elusive. Often motivated more by anxiety than discernment, efforts at change become driven by survival rather than empowered by missional purpose. Further, change for its own sake is usually self-defeating. Discontent with present realities is an insufficient motivation to form the creative and lasting changes in the church that can embrace a promising future. That requires, fundamentally, a fresh, spiritual, self-emptying engagement with the movement of God's mission in the world.

As authors of this book, the work of our lives has been devoted to understanding and nurturing congregations and the wider denominational structures to which they belong. We have reflected theologically on the church's life and calling and have been actively involved in the responsibilities of pastoral and administrative leadership. We've also shared widely in ecumenical settings, learning the splendid diversity of approaches to the ministry, mission, and governance of the church.

In all this work, spanning decades, we have each asked the simple question "How do churches change?" We've largely rejected the simplistic formulas and strategies that seem to abound. Our preoccupation has been with how to change the organizational culture of the institutional church, how to discover pathways to change that have an enduring impact, and how to root all efforts at change in God's missional purposes, not only for the church but for the world.

We've discovered fundamental things that we want to share, believing that in any process of transformative congregational and denominational change, certain basic features and practices must be present. First, the purpose must be clear, rooted in a missional thirst for God's desired future. Second, space for seeking such change must be opened creatively, free from the constraints of the normal governing process. Third, the procedures of decision-making must be grounded more in spiritual discernment than in strategic planning and parliamentary-style practices. Fourth, an open, invitational engagement in the biblical story, connecting it to the church's present journey—what we call Dwelling in the Word—must permeate all that is done. Fifth, the journey of faithful, missional change can happen only in partnership with others in the body of Christ, undertaken intentionally with other congregations and denominations seeking to travel these pathways together.

In sum, we are convinced that churches must change the way we change. Our experience convinces us that this is possible, based on the failures and the surprising discoveries that we have witnessed in the journeys of transformational change in the life and mission of the church, both in the United States and throughout the world. We're not providing some formula of "six simple steps to revitalize the church," because we don't believe they exist. Rather, we are offering tested practices and pathways that create a climate and a culture in which transformational, missional change can take root in the life of God's people.

CHAPTER ONE

What Needs to Change, and How?

More often than not, anxiety and discontent drive the perceived need for change. While these are necessary preconditions to change, they alone do not create sufficient energy for the missional change we are proposing in this book. Such change compels a church to place its commitment to participate in God's ongoing mission in the world at the heart of its life and identity. Anxiety and discontent are a place to begin, but moving to a process of spiritual discernment focused on the question of God's preferred and promised future is necessary to reveal both what needs to change and how those changes can be made.[1] We will start with an example at the denominational level to demonstrate this shift from managing anxiety and discontent to spiritually seeking deep missional change.

Recently a group of church leaders in a major European denomination were gathered at the invitation of the theological faculty of one of the denomination's major historical universities and the provider of theological education for most of its clergy for many centuries. At the table were chief executives of national church organizations, midgoverning judicatories, local churches— including some large, independent (so-called free church) leaders—and members of their parliament, and thought leaders in and out of the academy. They admitted, when asked, that this was an extremely rare meeting since their only purpose was not to conduct church business but to explore how churches change and how they need to be a part of that change process.

They were gathered not so much to act out of their hierarchical work roles but as perceived leaders who wanted a chance to explore in a relatively safe space the challenge they were feeling. Simply put: they knew that most of their local churches needed to change. Further, they knew that a critical mass of local church leaders felt the same need to change, but most of those local church leaders were unclear about what exactly needed to change and how that necessary change would happen. They agreed that greater church attendance or "more young persons" was desirable but that their absence was more a symptom than a cause. Even the "successful" free-church pastor who had significant ties to American mega-church leaders admitted that his local church was outside the norm and that he was not prepared to give a formula for what needed to change or how. Each of the attendees had ideas, hints, hunches, and some models of change that they had experienced or at least taken a workshop on or read about in a business, change-management setting. They all spoke of "spiritual" challenges both personally and organizationally and had various resources. What distinguished this meeting from those of other similar groups that we have experienced in the past thirty-some years was a genuine recognition and willingness to say in the presence of their fellow church leaders: we know we face a life-and-death crisis; we know we need to change; we know we don't know exactly what needs to change or how to do it.

Notice there are three very distinct attitudes and beliefs present in the group gathered. First, they know they face a life-and-death crisis. Second, they believe they need to change and that some change could make a difference. Third, however urgent the sense for change is within a leadership group, they believe they don't know exactly what needs to change or how to do it. We have often found only parts of these three prerequisites present in churches that say they want to change. Often, churches substitute big, hairy, audacious goals or catchy taglines that use contemporary phrasing, believing this will motivate the change they need. These tactics seldom generate the kind of energy necessary to make missional change.

Be that as it may, we find that the chance for successful missional change, the sort of change we are speaking of in this book, increases greatly when all three prerequisites are present. While we have seen churches pull off significant missional change without all of these prerequisites, we have observed a high correlation between successful missional change and the strong presence of all three prerequisites.

By *strong presence*, we mean at least three levels of presence. First, the behavior of the group reveals these three prerequisites; even if the group of leaders and greater community are not aware of them, they are present in their behavior. Second, a small group of leaders consciously seeks to create the time and space for these three prerequisites to become the behavior of the group. Third, 15 to 20 percent of the most active members of the church are attentive and focused on acting according to these three prerequisites. Let's review the prerequisites in a bit more detail.

A Matter of Life and Death for the Community

Often leaders develop this prerequisite experience indirectly rather than straightforwardly. I (Pat) remember working with a number of churches in the Dallas area. They were very independent local churches that had chosen to do something quite unusual for them: to deliberately learn with one another how to innovate local missional churches.

One local church had just spent millions of dollars adding onto and improving their campus under the general belief that "if we build it, they will come." They didn't come. The leadership of the local church sought to work with us because they wanted to be able to attract those for whom they had expanded their facilities. While the church had a relatively large worship attendance and there was high involvement in the various ministries of the congregation, the leaders had some sense that they needed a turnaround, or their present circumstances would reverse quickly.

The recognition of this need for turnaround came in part by observing that the median age of active participants was going up at an alarmingly increasing rate. More often than not, the increasing age of church members is the first publicly noted concern. Somehow it is safer to speak of the failure of a church to attract the young than it is to note many other symptoms of death. Among liberal mainline churches, the next most likely topic is a failure to reach persons of color, or persons of other language groups, or persons who live in poverty or whose sexual identity is other than the traditional norms. Among more conservative churches, we have found indicators like biblical illiteracy, low adult conversion, and diminishing worship attendance as publicly articulated indicators for concern.

From the perspective of this book, all of these are serious indicators but do not bring the deep missional crisis out into the open. Our use of the term "missional" deliberately shows our debt to the conversation begun by Lesslie Newbigin and David Bosch that notes the deep shifts in the relationship between church and wider culture in the modern period.[2] Following that missional conversation, we see the crisis at the level of culture, the deep values and beliefs that no longer match up between church and much of Western culture. We summarize the resulting notion of church as missional under four characteristics:

1. God is a missionary God who sends the church into the world.
2. God's mission in the world points to and participates in the reign of God.
3. The missional church is incarnational in contrast to attractional. This changes the dynamic of the church, both local and international, in this new missional era.
4. The internal life of the missional church focuses on every believer engaging in mission in their everyday life.[3]

Indeed, too often, conflict over various causes for concern deflects from an honest conversation regarding the life-and-death character of the challenge facing the church. Taking these indicators seriously means placing them in a system of priorities that puts the deeper missional crisis at the center. This requires a critical leadership—critical both in terms of the percentage of active members who recognize the deeper crisis and in terms of their ability to maintain a clear sense of the crisis and keep it central amid tremendous complexity. Navigating this complexity requires discernment and risk.

The critical mass required to address a church's deep missional crisis seems to be 15 to 20 percent of the active membership who recognize the crisis and commit to working toward substantive change, knowing they are in it for the long haul. Quick fixes will not be sufficient, though the church may need some to keep the momentum for deep missional change.

In the context of a local church, one usually cannot begin with the 15 to 20 percent. Our experience shows that if just 2 percent is willing to act over a three- to five-year period toward meeting the adaptive, missional challenge, the critical mass will develop. Note, however, that it is easy to attract those people who want change for change's sake but who bore at the sustained work of three to five years. Start with two people in one hundred who are willing to enter a process of spiritual discernment regarding God's preferred and promised future, and you are more likely to engage, attract, and form a critical mass of leaders. Much more on this spiritual discernment process later.

One other very important insight, which we will also discuss in much more detail, relates to the role of conflict in change. Change creates conflict. Conflict can be the Holy Spirit calling the church to multiply its mission. Conflict can be, at one and the same time, the work of the devil to create havoc and distrust, leaving the faithful divided, hurt, angry, disappointed, even despondent.

Once the critical mass of leadership is reached, it is essential to move the conversation from one that focuses primarily on managing anxiety and discontent to a journey of spiritual discernment seeking God's preferred and promised future. Although we will return to this theme of discerning God's preferred and promised future in greater detail, please note that rather than focusing on our preferences, we seek to discern God's preferences. Further, it is more about the future than either the present or the past. More, much more, later. Both of us know how difficult this shift is to accomplish. A proverbial line comes to mind: "It is hard to remember that your initial purpose was to drain the swamp when you are so busy beating off alligators." Indeed, one must manage the anxiety and discontent but keep the focus of energy, even the energy that is generated by the anxiety and discontent, on asking, "What is God up to here? What is God's preferred and promised future?" Frankly, the capacity to keep this focus separates the business of managing from the business of leading. Both are essential, but to bring about the kind of change necessary to meet the present challenges requires the capacity to lead, not just manage.

Management and Innovation, Together but Different

When a critical leadership group gathers outside the church's usual governing process, vaguely aware of the life-and-death character of their situation and honest about their not knowing what precisely they need to change but committed to change, Christian innovation becomes a possibility. **Christian innovation is a process starting in failure, growing out of a Christian imagination, and leading to a shared positive outcome.** We borrow from previous scholarship and best practices of over forty years of innovation in various spheres of change models. Chief among the movers and shakers in this area are Peter Senge, Ron Heifetz, and Everett Rogers. Senge harnessed an emerging systems theory from the social sciences and change models in business into his book *The Fifth Discipline*. Heifetz brought together models of government and business change in *Leadership without Easy Answers*. Rogers's research gathered profound insights into how innovation is diffused in traditional cultures. What all three men share is a sense that there are times when attending to organizational change is insufficient. Rather, the deep values of a culture that fund the various societal and organizational systems need to be drawn upon to innovate a shared positive outcome. Such change involves tremendous risk, and this risk involves failure.

We formed our understanding of innovation by marrying these insights to the Christian imagination, especially the Christian narrative of reconciliation in Jesus Christ. Put perhaps too simply, since risk, experimentation, and failure are essential to innovation and failure causes deep hurt, harm, and conflict, Christians draw upon the deeper resources of reconciliation in Jesus Christ. Within this enduring pattern of Christian life, the church can dare to risk and to fail, depending on God's promised mercy and forgiveness. While this attitude may initially appear as escapism to the sweet by-and-by, it actually draws on very specific, concrete, and time-tested practices of Christian innovation apparent in Scripture and in the emerging history of the church's life together.

Missional Change: Beyond Attraction to God's Mission in the World

One of the critical questions leaders of missional change must ask repeatedly is "What time is it?" We propose in this book that we are in a missional era, a very different time than what has been the norm for centuries in Western Christianity, or what some scholars call Christendom. While in some places, local churches still enjoy the leftovers of the local culture and society supporting and urging church membership and attendance, most local churches no longer enjoy that societal and cultural pressure in their favor. In addition, not only have lower birth rates negatively impacted the many traditional churches that fill their pews mostly with the children of members, but also massive demographic changes have occurred since 1965. Add the realities of increased individualism and the loss of a civil society that once strongly supported and worked with local churches and the systems that care about them. Along with these societal patterns, something we call "practical atheism" has crept into many local congregations, such that individuals certainly believe that God exists and is active in their lives, but when asked to tell stories to their fellow members about those everyday lives, they rarely use "God" as a subject in sentences with active verbs. In short, though members believe in God and God's movement in the world, they seldom—indeed, often never—articulate God's movement in their everyday lives to others. Combined with social and cultural changes, this practical atheism makes forming Christian community in a post-Christendom setting almost impossible; certainly, it is unlikely.

One major response to the challenges of post-Christendom—and one that has had clear success—could be described broadly as the attractional response. This model in one way or another assumes that if local churches and the systems that support them carry on certain ministries and programs, persons will be attracted

to those local churches and systems. Megachurches—
that is, churches with over two thousand active members—certainly give evidence to the effectiveness of
this approach. Both of us have had significant working
relationships with dozens of megachurches and have
found, in most cases, that they are extraordinary Christian communities. They demonstrate that there are
many people who are seeking effective, faithful, and
efficient programs and ministries. Many small house
churches work on the attractional model as well. They,
too, demonstrate a powerful presence of the church in
this post-Christendom setting. Many small churches remain vital Christian communities primarily through attracting membership. The underlying assumption for all
these different forms of local church remains attracting
people to join the local church. Whether they articulate it
or not, the churches assume that the local public communities within which they are situated are watching them
and that some might be attracted to them. Surely there
is some evidence that they are also building community
with those who are not Christian. However, the over-
whelming evidence shows that megachurches attract
mainly Christians who have been associated with other
local churches in their lives. Many house churches and
small churches follow the same pattern. The key distinc-
tion we want to make here, in speaking of *missional*, is
the church's move to joining God in God's mission in the

local community and to forming Christian community with those who are participating in some critical aspect of God's mission in their community.

In this new missional era of the Western church, certain essential practices deep within the DNA of the early church and abundantly working within the church of the two-thirds world today need to be rediscovered and embraced. We find that Saint Augustine of Hippo articulated one such primal practice in his *Confessions*. In analyzing his own circumstances, he recognizes how God continues to create a good world for us to love. Humans remain lovers, no matter how powerfully evil and sin pervert that deep need to love. Further, God continues to give us so many good things to do. But if we seek to love everything that is good, we diffuse our lives into nothingness. (*Nothingness* is one of Augustine's chief ways of describing evil.) Further, he notes that when we seek to love all things good, our love becomes disorderly, which he understands as sin. If we seek to do every good thing that can be done, we diffuse our lives into nothingness, evil, and disorderly love, sin. In this time after Christendom, the church local and ecumenical needs to compile short lists, not longer lists, of things to love and good things to do. Such creating of short lists requires the exercise of spiritual disciplines long neglected. Augustine suggests beginning with one activity: "Seek first the kingdom of God, and all will be given to you."

This present book provides both spiritual practices for and theological reflection on doing precisely that simple task. We summarize that practice as seeking to discern God's preferred and promised future for each local church and the systems that care about them. Put baldly, it is to recognize that we must begin with the end in mind: God's promised future that at the name of Jesus, every knee shall bow and every tongue confess him as Lord. How God will accomplish that promised future is very unclear in our time, just as it has been throughout the entire history of God's people. However, any Christian discerner who does not begin with that end in mind cannot put first things first in the here and now but, rather, diffuses his or her love into nothingness and disorderly love. In the meantime, we must discern penultimate goods to love and good things to do. These penultimate goods and good things are what we mean by God's *preferred* future that stands immediately before us now and God's *promised* future that continues to lure and shape our present in Christ, by the power of the Holy Spirit of our risen and ascended Lord, in the will of the Father of our Lord Jesus Christ, from the beginning to the end.

CHAPTER TWO

Making Space

The bus trip from Leipzig to Berlin takes about three hours. One thousand delegates to the General Council of the World Communion of Reformed Churches, who had arrived in Leipzig three days earlier, coming from two hundred different Reformed denominations from around the world, had to leave very early on buses on a Sunday morning to be at a nationally televised worship service in the Berliner Dom, the national Protestant cathedral of Germany.

I (Wes) was tired and needed coffee. I thought I'd nap. But an extraverted, engaging man from South Africa found me and said he wanted to talk on the bus ride to Berlin. He was Nelus Niemandt, a delegate to the General Council from the Dutch Reformed Church of South Africa and a leader in that denomination, twice serving as moderator of its General Synod. Nelus told me how he was a good friend of Pat Keifert, this book's coauthor, and how Pat's work had a deep impact in introducing missional transformation to many of their congregations and the wider denominational system.

Nelus wanted to talk about how churches change—both congregations and denominational systems. He had thought about this a lot and had put into practice experiments promoting transformational, missional change. After traveling to the Willow Creek leadership conferences in the US and then personally seeking out authors like Leonard Sweet and Brian McLaren, Nelus came across Pat Keifert's work with Church Innovations Institute. This connected deeply to Nelus's experience, as well as to his thirst for innovative models of change that had a solid basis in research and that deeply engaged the complex organizational cultures of church systems.

Nelus and I talked for much of the bus trip to Berlin, comparing experiences in attempting to introduce deep, missional change to our denominational systems—the Dutch Reformed Church of South Africa and the Reformed Church in America. Nelus stressed the essential need to "disrupt" the normal functioning of these systems if deep change were ever to have any chance of taking root. His experience as a denominational insider was that the combination of the rules of polity and order and a strong focus on results and outcomes severely constricted the room needed for the missional imagination that was essential to any meaningful change.

In such a situation, it was essential that there be creative leadership that would do three things. First, it had to disrupt existing patterns of governance to make space for new, emerging possibilities. Second, such leaders had to encourage novelty even though it could create more uncertainty in the system. And third, such leaders had to be able to identify new realities and "make sense" in complex situations that often became filled with uncertainty and even conflict. In that task, narrative language, images, and metaphors became key to discovering a fresh future. Such leadership stood in contrast to the more common leadership patterns of promoting strategic planning, task orientation, and predictive results.

Nelus Niemandt, in fact, had researched and written about all this in a chapter titled "Complex Leadership and Missional Transformation" for the book *The End of Leadership? Leadership and Authority at Crossroads*,[4] which was just about to be published in Europe when he and I were together in Germany. He used the Dutch Reformed Church in South Africa as a case study, and his analysis was intriguing. Nelus also drew on other research to show how transformational leaders "play a role in destabilizing systems by disrupting existing processes or patterns of behavior."[5] This underscores how transformational change can emerge in church systems only when intentional space is created that breaks from the normal patterns of business, governance, and organizational life.

"Disruption" is not the usual activity expected of church leaders, among whom stability and order are the preferred operational styles. But in one way or another, disruption is usually essential for lasting change. And such actions should be thought of as creative rather than iconoclastic. Whether in a congregation, regional governing body, or general assembly, the normal life of church systems is governed by a desire for predictability. Routines are valued. It's expected that meetings end on time. The decisions involved in governance are funneled into an orderly process of doing business. Such processes are fine for maintaining church organizations. But to accomplish transformational change, they must be disrupted. Space must be created if something new is to emerge.

As the bus rolled on down the autobahn toward Berlin, I related to Nelus my attempts to make space for transformational change in the Reformed Church in America. Coming as an "outsider" to be general secretary and encouraged by the search committee to discover a vision for the RCA's future, I had little idea of how to proceed. But it was clear that this denomination in the Reformed tradition was overgoverned, with multiple layers of boards charged with overlapping decision-making.

A body called the General Synod Council, made up of about sixty members, met three times a year, between the annual meetings of the General Synod. Its workbook was thick, full of reports written by staff and other boards, and prepared every three months. Council members tried to read, understand, and make intelligent comments, but it often seemed like a periodic firehose of information, with staff trying to make sure their good work was documented and justified. Space for asking "big questions" and thinking creatively about the future was absent.

At my first General Synod Council meeting in September 1994, I offered a novel idea. For the next meeting in January, why not discard the workbook entirely and go to a retreat center in Arizona. The only assignment would be to read the book of Acts—that would be the workbook. Council members, I suggested, would find time to reflect on the life of the RCA, interact more personally with one another, create a climate infused by worship, and think about our future as a denomination. Because I was brand-new as general secretary, the council agreed.

The time at the Franciscan Renewal Center in Paradise Valley, with a view of Camelback, was fruitful. Mostly, it created an experience that disrupted the normal pattern of governance and introduced a novel way for the General Synod Council members to be together. A host of fresh questions found room for expression. A facilitated process with small groups yielded refreshing ideas about the future. A new discussion was begun.

This retreat time in Arizona opened the way for a search process for a future vision for the Reformed Church in America. For this denomination, nearly four hundred years old, that was a new and unique experience. Such a vision got described as "a compelling picture of God's desired future." It took two more years of determined work, performed while normal business received the necessary attention. A retreat by a commissioned small group held at St. Benedict's Monastery in Snowmass, Colorado, finalized words that were to have a lasting impact on the RCA's denominational system and its congregations:

> The Reformed Church in America is a fellowship of congregations called by God and empowered by the Holy Spirit to be the very presence of Jesus Christ in the world.
>
> Our shared task is to equip congregations for ministry—a thousand churches in a million ways doing one thing—following Christ in mission in a lost and broken world so loved by God.

Those two sentences took on a life of their own, becoming a fresh lens for rethinking denominational activities and being embraced and interpreted by local congregations. They opened avenues for missional theology to impact a fresh understanding of the church and began conversations about transformational change. The last two sentences of what became known as the "Mission and Vision Statement" identified the change of organizational culture, and the permission for disruption, which were essential:

> To live out this vision by consistories, classes, synods, and staff, our decision-making will be transformed by a pervasive climate of worship, discernment, and biblical reflection. We will no longer do business as usual, nor our usual business.

All this became a template to guide directions, inform ways of approaching business, and identify key questions impacting the RCA's future. Eventually it led to a ten-year goal named "Our Call," which developed specific priorities with projected activities and outcomes. In some ways, this evolved into a system of control and predictability, which Nelus Niemandt had warned against. But transformational change goes in cycles, from disruption to new space, generating novel ideas and widespread uncertainty, to a framing that makes sense and identifies a new future, followed by a reorganization of resources and activities, which then get systemized, accomplishing desired ends, but eventually needing to be disrupted again.

None of this can happen, however, without making fresh space within the normal routines of business and governance.

When a church group, be it a congregation or a broader denominational body, embarks on this journey, they will enter "liminal space." This comes from the Latin word *limen*, which means "threshold." It describes the experience of leaving the certainties of the past behind but not yet knowing the shape of what is to come. Thus, it is a space filled with questions, anxieties, ambiguity, and uncertainty. But dwelling in this space is essential for transformational change.

The concept of liminality is often used by therapists and others in helping individuals understand transitions in their personal journeys. Some simple examples can explain. Both of us writing this book have made major moves recently. I (Wes) and my wife, Karin, had lived for a decade in Grand Rapids, Michigan, with its cohesive culture, supported by a local church and all the networks associated with my work as RCA general secretary and Karin's as a hospital chaplain. We decided to move to Santa Fe, New Mexico, drawn by its landscape and diverse cultures, but where we knew only two people.

Pat Keifert and his wife, Dr. Jeanette Keifert, had lived comfortably for decades in the Twin Cities of Minnesota, with a historical culture similar to Grand Rapids. Luther Seminary had been Pat's educational home since he began teaching there in 1980, and Jeanette served as a family-practice physician in the area for three decades. Approaching the threshold of retirement, they decided to move to Red Lodge, Montana. This city of 2,300, with trout-filled Rock Creek running through town, is located at the base of Beartooth Pass, which leads to the Lamar Valley of Yellowstone National Park.

Both Karin and I, and Pat and Jeanette, entered liminal space when making this transition. In fact, when Karin and I had recently arrived in Santa Fe, we met new friends, a Lutheran clergy couple. When Karin described how we had left a stable life in Grand Rapids and arrived in Santa Fe, where so much seemed uncertain and unknown, our new friends replied, "Oh, so you're in liminal space." It was, in fact, the first time Karin or I had heard the term. But it described perfectly our experience at the time.

Embarking on various kinds of journeys—psychological, spiritual, relational, and geographical—necessitates moving away from past certainties. The new that is desired cannot be discovered unless the old is released and left behind. But the challenge is that one must live in this liminal space before the new can be fully discovered and embraced. It takes time, patience, courage, and discernment to discover the content of a next chapter, and that can't happen if you are clinging to the old. One can think of liminal space as that point when a trapeze performer has let go of one bar while anxiously waiting to grab hold of the next.

The well-known Franciscan author Richard Rohr puts it this way:

We have to allow ourselves to be drawn into sacred space, into liminality. All transformation takes place here. We have to allow ourselves to be drawn out of "business as usual" and remain patiently on the "threshold" . . . where we are betwixt and between the familiar and the completely unknown. There alone is our old world left behind, while we are not yet sure of the new existence. That's a good place where genuine newness can begin.[6]

Church organizations embarking on a journey of transformational change must also expect to be drawn into liminal space. But that's often resisted. Addicted to predictability and control, church leaders often desire change processes to be smooth and orderly, a step-by-step program: Write a new mission statement in three months. Do a "SWOT" analysis and develop a strategic plan in the following three months. Establish goals and determine measurable outcomes in the following three months. Then rewrite position descriptions of staff and evaluate their performance according to those outcomes. Present it all for approval to the church council or denominational governing board, completed in less than a year. Those writing this book, who have each worked with congregations and denominational systems for thirty years, have never seen transformational change happen that way.

Church organizations desiring to discover and embrace deep change that will unite them with more abandon to God's missional purposes in the world need spiritual preparedness more than strategic planning. They must expect to be led into liminal space just as certainly as the people of Israel spent their time in the wilderness after leaving the enslaving realities of Egypt and before entering the promised land. True change happens only by creating open space in organizational life through intentional intervention and then expecting the unexpected of liminal space. That's where a fresh encounter with God's Spirit is most likely to occur.

As one thinks about any process of change within congregations or denominational structures that has made a lasting difference, this pattern of disruption in the normal routine of business and governance, and the experience of liminal space, can probably be identified, whether deliberately planned or not. This is a pattern of events that seems to happen one way or another. When it's not anticipated or consciously initiated, the disruption in the system will come in potentially destructive ways—angry encounters, unexpected resignations, and prolonged business meetings that seem only to increase frustration. Then, the entry into liminal space creates far more anxiety in the system and multiplies feelings of mistrust. That's why a process of change in a relatively healthy system should forecast and structure ways to make fresh space that interrupts normalcy and expects the experience of being led into liminal uncertainty.

Examples of how this works abound. An early case in the life of a well-known, pioneering congregation, the Church of the Saviour in Washington, DC, is worth pondering. In many ways, Church of the Saviour was an outlier among US congregations, founded by Gordon and Mary Cosby shortly after World War II. Convinced that congregations should be organized around the disciplined commitment of their members to inner spiritual growth and an outward journey, with a mandatory involvement in external mission, Gordon structured the church around "mission groups." Each group was called to a specific expression of costly involvement to address society's needs, hungers, and injustices. These groups were also a means of corporate fellowship and accountability. To those who think about ecclesiology, *koinonia* and *diaconia* were merged intrinsically and inseparably together at the core of what it meant to belong to this congregation. This is rarely the case in churches.

The result was an impressive number of innovative outreach ministries of caring and justice, like a coffee-house, low-cost housing ventures, job mentoring, empowerment of children, health clinics and initiatives, and much more, as well as a retreat farm to nurture contemplative practices and spiritual growth. Membership required a series of classes, involvement as an "intern member" in a mission group, and a high commitment of one's time, money, and devotion, totaling two years of preparation. The church functioned with a relatively small number of full members—about one hundred—with others serving as intern members or exploring on the fringes.

The church grew. But for Church of the Saviour, that became a problem. Gordon became convinced that the model of this church, with its strong communal nature, high relational quality, and dependence on his vision, preaching, and pastoring, could not endure as membership grew. He felt that the essence that made the Church of the Saviour unique and vital would get lost as numbers increased beyond a certain point and that the church's dependence on his own role and gifts had to be broken.

The questions seemed right, but no answers were clear. And there was no way to process this within the normal structure of the church's governance, with a council and several mission groups. A means of intervention came from a proposal, backed by Gordon, to establish a New Land Committee. Fed by the biblical metaphor of the people of Israel's journey to the promised land, this group was charged with discovering the way to the future, hopefully without forty years in the wilderness.

Grounded in spiritual practices, the group met in conversations, reflecting and listening for about a year, and then went on a retreat. Much of that time was marked by silence as they sought to make sense of and find direction through all the questions and issues that had bubbled to the surface. During that time on retreat, the group had its own experience of liminal space as it began to let go of decades of history and familiar structures, while barely imagining what could come next.

The result was a proposal that the Church of the Saviour intentionally divide itself into several "sister communities," which would be smaller versions of the original congregation, each with its own pastoral leadership. They would function with autonomy but remain loosely linked together in fellowship. Emerging in some cases out of existing mission groups, each new community would have a specific point of focus, or charism. While Gordon's preaching and teaching through the years would leave a lasting imprint, he would no longer share pastoral responsibility for the whole.

The proposal was greeted first with appreciation and excitement, but then with anxiety and critique. What was being left behind seemed obvious and, in some cases, painful and threatening. But what was proposed seemed ambiguous and uncertain. Now the congregation as a whole was anticipating liminal space. Some members couldn't imagine Gordon not being pastorally central to their lives and to the whole community. Others doubted the viability of such sister communities, wondering how they could be established and sustained.

In the journey of the Church of the Saviour, what most supported the transition to a new future was the common depth of shared spiritual practice. Tools existed, long honed, for encountering "the dark night of the soul" and the times of doubt that accompany any growth in faith. Those habits of the heart sustained most members amid this critical transition. Anxiety and mistrust were certainly present but were tempered by deep wisdom and discerning insight.

Through this transition, thirteen sister communities eventually emerged. All this happened in the 1970s. Decades later, some still exist, while others have withered. More transitions have marked the church's journey. But a legacy endures—namely, the spawning of over a hundred outreach ministries throughout these decades, and an impact on the understanding of what it means to be the church that has touched tens of thousands, especially through the writings of the late Elizabeth O'Connor. The Church of the Saviour was a "missional church" through and through before the term was even invented. It changed and flourished through the pattern of disruption, spiritually infused imagination of a preferred future, and discernment that brought trustworthy direction to a climate of uncertainty.

Crucial to this pattern of disruption, imagination, uncertainty, and transformational change is how we understand time. This chapter's title, "Making Space," identifies the first chief obstacle: our lack of "time," because of the crowdedness of our normal processes of governance, whether in a congregation or a denominational system. The Church of the Saviour was a single, small congregation struggling with its future. At the other end of the ecclesial spectrum is the Vatican, responsible for the congregations comprising one-half of the world's Christians.

As you walk into St. Peter's Square, in front of St. Peter's Basilica, the plaza is shaped more like an oval. Colonnades stretch out in a semicircular fashion, designed by Bernini to welcome the visitor like the maternal arms of the mother church. The main entrance into St. Peter's Square, opposite the basilica, is from Via della Conciliazione (The Road of Conciliation), which connects St. Peter's Square with the Castel Sant'Angelo. Shops, offices, museums, and churches are on the sides of this broad, straight boulevard.

A short way down from the entrance to St. Peter's Square on the Via della Conciliazione are the offices of the Pontifical Council for Promoting Christian Unity. This is the center of the Vatican's efforts to build bridges toward Christian unity and to coordinate all the official involvement of the Catholic Church at the global level in various ecumenical organizations and initiatives. The president of the council is Cardinal Kurt Koch, who comes from Switzerland. Bishop Brian Ferrell is the secretary, and staff from a variety of countries and cultures carry out its work.

In Switzerland, the trains are punctual, to the minute. When you stand on a train platform in Geneva to board a train for Zurich scheduled to depart at 10:54 a.m., the train pulls into the station and departs at 10:54 a.m. Swiss culture is shaped by such timeliness, and its precision watches have a worldwide reputation for being the most reliable and accurate.

Cardinal Koch, a warm and committed person, wears a Swiss watch. The story is told how he will come to staff meetings, exactly on time, looking at his watch, and displeased when others are not punctual. For him, meetings begin and end on schedule, to be efficient. On one occasion, a staff member from another culture, sensing Cardinal Koch's frustration, said to him, "Cardinal, you have a watch. We have time."

Similar stories are told in other cross-cultural settings where different understandings of time, schedules, and expectations come into conflict. American culture has invented the phrase "making time," regarding time as a commodity to be manufactured, controlled, and allocated. When we say we "don't have time," that is not accurate. And obviously, no one can ever "make time." What is at stake is how we value and attach importance to certain activities as opposed to others.

Of course, no one can argue against keeping a calendar, having appointments, and organizing one's activities. But this is the framework that most of us, especially if we are from Western, white cultures, impose on the life of our churches. Whether it's a congregation or a denominational structure, we commodify and control time. That becomes a dominant and often subconscious value. For running meetings well and getting home on time, this works fine. But not for a process of spiritually rooted, missional transformation.

Change is not punctual.

A journey of transformational change begins by disturbing the normal processes of maintaining order and governance. This opens up space to allow prophetic and spiritual imagination to find room, and even flourish. And such a climate should not be foreign to the life of the church. In truth, just a cursory reading of the book of Acts reveals a continual pattern of unexpected interventions of the Spirit of God, which create unforeseen possibilities for the emerging church's life, witness, and mission.

Our efficient, business-minded culture teaches us to tame time. We would do well to remember that the ancient Greek language of the New Testament has two words for time. One is *chronos*, referring to the chronological, sequential nature of time commonly thought of today in Western culture. The other is *kairos*, meaning the right, opportune moment, filled with special significance and meaning. Chronos can be tamed, measured, and controlled. Kairos invites us to suspend those activities in the face of wonder, discovery, and revelation.

Every seminary student has learned about these two words, and parishioners have probably heard them mentioned in sermons. But the applications have been mostly theological, referring to kairos moments of God's intervention in salvation history, interrupting the normal progression of time and history as chronos. That is fine, but the application of these two views of time shouldn't stop there. The contrast between chronos and kairos also takes place with the ongoing life of the body of Christ, in congregational committee meetings and denominational conference rooms.

The organizational culture of congregations and denominational systems is dominated by a chronos understanding of time. Transformational change, recentered on participation in God's ongoing mission in the world today, requires expecting and embracing moments of kairos when our life together is intersected by a holy wonder and spiritual discovery. Space for imagining God's preferred future is then at hand. And the shared journey can begin to move forward, often to unexpected destinations.

CHAPTER THREE

Nurturing a Climate of Discernment

In 1997 the *Harvard Business Review* published an article titled "Changing the Way We Change."[7] More than two decades later, it remains insightful and relevant. Its authors were examining the attempts of three massive organizations—Sears, Royal Dutch Shell, and the US Army—to make fundamental changes. The attempt was to get beyond just making changes in structures and activities to nurturing transformational change. From these studies, the article came to conclusions about the challenge facing these organizations and any others on this path, noting that "the 800-pound gorilla that impaired performance and stifled change was culture." Fundamental transformation had to engage changes in organizational culture.

It's natural for those shaped by the classic American institutions built in the 1950s and 1960s to believe that needed change in an organization comes through altering structures, job descriptions, and quantifiable goals. Such change can be engineered, managed, and controlled.

There's a trust in the organization's fundamental ability to function according to its methods of governance and its historic capacities. Simply changing how its structures are put together and sharpening its goals, it is believed, will increase efficiency, strengthen performance, and solve most challenges.

What the authors from the *Harvard Business Review* discovered, however, was that the more fundamental changes needed and desired by organizations would not come through such means. Rather, what they called the "culture" of the organization had to be engaged and transformed to yield the type of change desired. At the time, that concept was new. But now it's become more widely accepted, at least rhetorically. Nurturing and practicing such changes in organizational culture, however, proves to be a formidable task.

All this applies deeply to churches. Recall how we began the book. The three prerequisites for beginning the process of transformational, missional change are (1) recognizing that we face a life-and-death situation, (2) knowing that deep change is essential (with a core of 10 to 20 percent of members convinced of this), and (3) not really knowing what needs to change or how to do it. The reason one typically encounters uncertainty about what needs to change is that changes in organizational culture are required but are hard to identify, and they typically raise anxiety when they are confronted.

To enter into this process, we need clarity about what is meant by three terms: *organizational culture*, *discernment*, and *consensus*.

First, organizational culture. One way of thinking about this is to simply note the formal and informal ways in which people relate to one another. Groups develop their norms, expectations, and styles of functioning. Some are reflected in formal structures of management and decision-making, while others are found in what is and is not acceptable in how people informally relate to one another.

This is particularly true of congregational and denominational systems. Often, these matters become ingrained and even unconscious. They are revealed in meetings of a congregational council when someone responds to a novel proposal by saying, "That's just not the way we do things here at First Methodist Church." An established "way of doing things" can comprise various behaviors and values, such as rationality, an orderly business process, prayers as "bookends" to contentious meetings, committee reports always being approved by the senior pastor before their presentation, a long-established order of worship, and much more. Such elements define an organizational culture.

More personally, such a culture also includes expected patterns of behavior within the church system. Articulations of faith and "trust in God" are a norm, while expressions of doubt make others uncomfortable.

A superficial confidence that "God is in charge" serves as an assumption that dilutes or represses more threatening assessments of a situation, particularly if one believes that life-and-death matters are at stake. Conflict and serious dissent are pushed underground. A common pattern is that honest reactions, fears, and judgments about a church meeting are expressed in the parking lot after its conclusion.

Our conviction is that prevailing systems of organizational culture in congregations and denominational systems can function adequately to maintain normalcy. People become adjusted and make concessions regarding their intuitions or apprehensions in order to comply with dominant expectations. But once a conviction is reached that a life-and-death situation, at least a long-term one, is facing a congregation or a whole denomination, and that some kind of transformational missional change is required, then organizational culture must be changed. Again, organizational culture is the eight-hundred-pound gorilla in the congregational council meeting or the denominational assembly.

Often, nothing characterizes and engrains an organizational culture in church systems more than its decision-making process. How things get decided is pivotal. And usually this dimension of church life seems to be on automatic pilot. We follow forms of *Robert's Rules of Order* and vote. A majority determines the result through a process of motions, debate, amendments, amendments to amendments, binary forms of choices (yes or no), and resulting decisions.

It's worth recalling the origin of this practice. The credit (or blame) goes to Brigadier General Henry Martyn Robert of the US Army Corps of Engineers. He graduated fourth in his class from West Point in 1857. At the beginning of the Civil War, he supervised the construction of fortifications around Washington, DC. But Robert was a Baptist. When asked, as a young man, to chair a meeting at a local Baptist church, it quickly spun out of his control into divisive arguments, to his great dismay.

On a later assignment to San Francisco, he served on the board of trustees of the First Baptist Church and on the board of the Young Men's Christian Association. Finding patterns of dispute and argument to be disabling, he turned to parliamentary methods of making decisions in political bodies and drafted his first, sixteen-page guide for societies and organizations. But that was insufficient, and in 1876 he published, at his own expense, the 176-page *Pocket Manual of Rules of Order for Deliberative Assemblies*. Designed so it could be carried in a coat pocket, it soon became widely used and was successively expanded and revised, becoming commonly known as *Robert's Rules of Order* to this day.

Several features about Robert and his rules should be noted. First, he was trained as a military leader. Systems of command and control were essential. Second, in the face of unruly arguments, he wanted to bring a means of order and control into the divisive settings he discovered in Baptist churches. Third, for his solution, he drew on parliamentary systems utilized in the political arena. In all this, Robert began by assuming that conflict was intrinsic and immobilizing, and that it needed to be controlled in church settings in similar ways as in political venues. So, a codified and complex system of debate eventually yielding to majority votes was established.

Thus, utilizing his military experience, Robert devised clear and detailed "rules" that would insure "order." He wanted church bodies to be governed by the same kind of systems of control, regulation, and predictability for outcomes that allowed him to oversee the design of the Galveston seawall following the disastrous hurricane of 1900.

It's fascinating to see how *Robert's Rules of Order* has acquired a status of respect, trust, and authority in numerous church bodies across denominational lines that is often second only to the Bible. The assumption is that this is the way the church must act to govern itself. Often there's almost a sacred and obligatory quality attached to following *Robert's Rules*. Frequently these rules are even enshrined in the constitutions or bylaws of church bodies. This becomes a determinative marker of organizational culture in the church.

In our view, it's astonishing that church bodies, from small congregations to major assemblies, hold *Robert's Rules of Order* nearly sacrosanct. The underlying assumption is that if you conduct "business" in a fashion that ensures rational control through military-style precision, treating all matters that arise as either-or propositions, using mechanisms created to deal with political decision-making, and progressing often with tedious detail toward a majority vote, even of just 51 percent, then you will discover the will of God. That is, or should be, the goal of decisions reached in church bodies—namely, how can God's Spirit lead us to an outcome we hope is responsive to God's intentions or God's will? To trust in *Robert's Rules of Order* as the vehicle to get us to that end is, frankly, preposterous.

Certainly we've all experienced situations where *Robert's Rules of Order* has been effective in helping a group come to a decision. This method is workable in many situations. But it assumes that there's a situation of conflict, seen in binary terms, and that a solution favored by a majority margin of even one will be acceptable and embraced by the whole body. When this is part of the organizational culture of a church, the result can be disastrous, often intensifying factions, deepening divisiveness, and equating the "winning" party as the one favored by God. It's a process that, in our view, quenches the work of God's Holy Spirit and reduces a church body to a politicized organization, often mirroring the dynamics and style of secular politics.

The word *discernment* does not appear in the newly revised edition of *Robert's Rules of Order*, which runs 669 pages, but that's the quality that is essential to any process of transformational, missional change in the life of the church. In fact, in our work with congregations and denominational bodies over three decades, we've never witnessed a process of deep transformation that has occurred when its form of governance has relied on the methodology of *Robert's Rules*. The form and style of decision-making need to change through nurturing a climate of discernment.

When seeking transformational, missional change, we've used the language of yearning to discover "God's preferred and promised future" for a given church body. This places the conversation in a different framework. We're not starting with concepts of strategic planning, priority setting, and resource allocation, although those may at points have a role. Rather, what captures this process verbally is the language of discernment.

This term has a long and varied religious history. Within Catholic circles, *discernment* has been often associated with the process of discovering one's vocational calling, such as to the priesthood. And in the past couple of decades, as the language and practices of spiritual formation in the Catholic tradition have bled into Protestant circles, *discernment* is frequently applied to the attempt to know one's specific calling.

The use of terms in books can be tracked using the Google Books Ngram Viewer. This tool finds that the use of the word *discernment* decreased consistently from 1800 until about 1990, when it began to start climbing back up. The increase reflects an emerging sense that a better vocabulary needs to be found to describe Christian experience and the life of its organized bodies.

Within Pentecostal and charismatic circles, "discerning the spirits" has special importance. As individual members exercise spiritual gifts in prophecy, tongues, and similar expressions, it is crucial to "discern" if these are truly from the Holy Spirit or not. In similar fashion, and in some evangelical communities as well, such discernment means sorting out right from wrong in expressions of doctrine and interpretation of Scripture.

The history of the term goes back to the early church, including some usage in the New Testament. Here the concept of spiritual discernment suggests the ability to comprehend matters in ways that go beyond natural practices. Romans 12:2 urges believers not be conformed to the world but to be transformed and renewed so they may "discern what is the will of God, what is good and acceptable and perfect."[8] The opening of the letter to the Philippians offers a prayer for the young church that includes these words: "that your love may abound more and more, with knowledge and all discernment, so that you may approve what is excellent, and so be pure and blameless for the day of Christ" (Phil. 1:9–10). The New Revised Standard Version translates the Greek term in this passage as "full insight."

In the writings of early church fathers, discernment receives further attention. Noteworthy for our purposes are the insights of John Cassian, who stresses the quality of humility, where one's judgments and actions are open to the insights and perceptions of others in the Christian community. Humility is the path that allows the seeking of a "common mind" within the body of Christ and that reflects the frequent New Testament admonitions to practice a unity that respects the diversity of gifts but joins all in bonds of love.

Today discernment means, even in secular parlance, the ability to understand matters in ways that go beneath the surface and to nurture judgments that reveal core truths. Similarly, in Christian terms, discernment is rooted in the ability to spiritually penetrate the meaning of events and the direction of the future. It cuts to the heart of things and apprehends the movement of God's Spirit. Moreover, it is nurtured, tested, and affirmed in the context of community.

Nurturing a climate of discernment in church bodies entails giving attention to three qualities: humility, intuition, and imagination. John Cassian, a fourth-century theologian, was right in echoing the injunctions of the New Testament to regard others as more important than ourselves and to hold our own convictions in healthy, suspended belief as we listen with an open heart to one another and to the promptings of God's Spirit. In such a climate, insights more often come at an intuitive level, where we sense and glean perceptions more than we attain rational certainties.

Additionally, within this climate, imagination should have room to flourish. Craig Dykstra, who headed the religion division of the Lilly Endowment for many years, supported persistent research on how to foster what he termed "pastoral excellence." At one point he identified two qualities most lacking and needed. The first was networks of peer relationships, which create trustworthy environments for support and growth. The second was "pastoral and ecclesial imagination." Nurturing this quality is essential for church bodies to thrive and is crucial to a climate of discernment.

Prayer, experiences of worship, and biblical reflection should be woven into this environment of discernment. However, the dominant practice in many church bodies is to segregate these spiritual experiences from the practical arenas where business is conducted and where decisions are made. Of course, meetings are opened and closed in prayer. Perhaps there's a biblical reflection at the start. Church assemblies typically begin with morning worship, often showcasing prominent preachers. But such spiritual practices are confined to specific places and rarely impact the cultural norms and practices of governance and decision-making. Nurturing a climate of discernment requires dismantling the walls that segregate places set apart for our encounter with God from places of our work of governance.

These ideas are not novel. Fortunately, there's a growing body of research, literature, and experience that explores methods for integrating the practice of spirituality with the work of governance. As early as 1995, Charles M. Olsen wrote *Transforming Church Boards into Communities of Spiritual Leaders*,[9] published by the Alban Institute. Olsen outlines four practices to convert traditional church boards into communities of spiritually grounded leaders: storytelling, biblical reflection, prayerful discernment, and visioning for the future. All of this is set forth in a framework called "worshipful work." That became the name of the center Olsen established in Kansas City to further this model in the life of the church. This imaginative initiative received financial support from the Lilly Endowment.

Olsen is a Presbyterian pastor, so he knows well the resistance to establishing such fresh methods in systems steeped in doing business "decently and in order." In 1997 he partnered with a Methodist, Danny Morris, to write *Discerning God's Will Together: A Spiritual Practice for the Church.*[10] It's a guide that helpfully elaborates the process and practice of discernment in five chapters, answering what, why, who, how, and where. Included is a suggested road map with ten steps, the goal of which is desiring to discover God's will, "nothing more, nothing less, nothing else." Their work takes note of various streams of Christian tradition, including John Cassian's contribution to discernment. For us, as authors of this book, the work of Morris and Olsen is not abstract; we've utilized elements of it in our consulting for and leadership of church bodies.

Meanwhile, new initiatives exploring alternatives in the prevailing culture of church governance and decision-making were taking root in Australia. In 1994 the Uniting Church of Australia selected its first woman moderator, Dr. Jill Tabart. She was dismayed with the "my way is the only answer, win at all costs" style of governance, rooted in parliamentary styles of debate and voting. Her convictions persuaded the church's National Assembly to take the risk of adopting new methods of decision-making rooted in careful listening, honest searching for God's guidance, and discovering forms of consensus. These fresh approaches, which changed the culture of the Uniting Church of Australia's National Assemblies, were embraced, developed, and began to be noticed in ecumenical circles.

The World Council of Churches was facing its own challenges around decision-making styles during that decade. For a variety of reasons, its Orthodox members had become increasingly unsettled with their role in the WCC. Their concerns seemed often to be marginalized, with an ecumenical agenda and style that wasn't sufficiently responsive, in their view, to the importance of Orthodox presence and participation in the WCC. These matters came to a head prior to the WCC's Eighth Assembly, held in Harare, Zimbabwe, in 1998. As a result, the assembly took the extraordinary step of appointing a Special Commission on Orthodox Participation in the WCC, made up equally of Orthodox and non-Orthodox members.

As they began to meet in the years following the assembly, one key concern, among others, that the Orthodox raised was the WCC's decision-making style. They could not fathom how the WCC's Central Committee could be governed by a parliamentary process in which decisions made by simple-majority voting, whereby just one vote could tip the scales, would be considered God's will for the way forward. Orthodox membership on this governing body was about 25 percent of the whole, so this also meant that a majority could overrule Orthodox perspectives on crucial issues that they might regard as essential to their foundational understanding of being a church, and therefore could affect their faithful participation in ecumenical life.

Other, non-Orthodox voices on the Special Commission also raised critiques about the WCC's decision-making style, which had been shaped by American and western European political systems, employing methods similar to *Robert's Rules of Order*. Eden Grace, from the Quaker community and a member of the WCC Central Committee as well, brought forward insights of long-practiced discernment and consensus in the decision-making culture of the Society of Friends. WCC members from Asia, Africa, and Latin America brought experiences of decision-making from their cultures, which relied far more on community building and sharing than on the oppositional, conflictive methods characterizing political and church bodies in Europe and the United States.

The Special Commission worked hard and well to develop a whole alternative style and method of decision-making for the WCC that moved away from its parliamentary style and fostered means of discernment and consensus. When its final report was adopted, covering many areas of Orthodox participation in the WCC's life, it included a section on embracing a consensus style of decision-making that would "enable representatives to have more 'space' to discern the will of God for the churches, the WCC and the wider human family." The purpose of the report was to recommend "a process for seeking the common mind of a meeting without deciding issues by means of voting." In the years since, the WCC adopted, embraced, and developed this fresh means of decision-making in its process of governance.

Attention to these developments in ecumenical circles was furthered when the WCC published a book by Jill Tabart in 2003, *Coming to Consensus: A Case Study for the Churches*. It explained the significant experience of the Uniting Church of Australia with this new process of governance and its applications elsewhere. When the World Alliance of Reformed Churches met for its General Council—a once-in-seven-years global assembly—in Accra, Ghana, in 2004, it also committed to change its decision-making style, and Dr. Tabart was there as a special adviser to their process. This was highly significant, since the WARC comprised most of the Presbyterian and Reformed denominations from around the world, many of which had integrated *Robert's Rules of Order* as part of their DNA.

In 2010 the WARC merged with the Reformed Ecumenical Council, becoming the World Communion of Reformed Churches. At its General Council meeting in Leipzig, Germany, in 2017, this discernment and consensus style of decision-making helped them deal harmoniously with the divisive issue of same-sex relationships, maintaining their unity. The communion no longer uses a win-lose style, with majorities imposing their will on minorities—a way of behaving in groups that is consistently rejected by every New Testament admonition regarding how those in the body of Christ are to relate to one another.

The description of how these global, long-established ecumenical bodies, containing a wide diversity of languages, cultures, and theologies, have transformed their process of decision-making is highly instructive for the wider church. When it is proposed that church bodies consider "changing the way they change" and imagining new ways of trying to discern God's will and make decisions, the first response is usually one of skepticism. The assumption is that it can't be done. The fact is, however, that it is being done by some of the most complex global church bodies that exist. And their experiences have been positive, leading to new developments in their organizational cultures. Since such methods have been successful and helpful with even the World Council of Churches meetings in Geneva, why shouldn't they at least be considered by the First Presbyterian Church of Wichita?

These examples raise the question of what is meant by *consensus*, the third term important to this discussion. Further, how does consensus relate to discernment?

First, consensus is often assumed to mean unanimity. That can be one result, but it's not the only way of expressing consensus. When groups have transitioned to a consensus style of decision-making, they often define options that are possible. Unanimity is one, in which all agree. Another is where the "mind of the meeting" seems clear from well-developed discussion, with all voices being heard; those remaining in disagreement (often a small number) give their consent for the matter to go forward, and opportunities for recording officially differing views are provided. Another option is that the matter under consideration is perceived as not ready for a decision and is postponed until further reflection, study, and discussion can take place. Finally, it can be the sense of the group that no agreement is possible on a given proposal, and it is withdrawn.

All these options fall within the framework of deciding matters by consensus rather than by majority vote with rigid, binary rules for debate. What becomes key are the gifts of those who moderate such a process. Further, a variety of methods can be used, such as providing those in a decision-making body with colored cards (green, yellow, and red, for instance) and asking them to express at several given times whether they are warm toward an idea (green), are not certain (yellow), or feel opposed (red). The moderator continually makes sure that all voices are being heard and keeps seeking the overall direction of the body, utilizing the show of cards and other means, in the course of its discussion.

Within smaller groups such as a church council, this process can be less formally organized, but the intent is the same. In larger denominational assemblies, key issues can be identified by an agreed-upon process and then discussed thoroughly in smaller groups in which all delegates participate. The results of those discussions are then interpreted by a steering group and shared together with the larger assembly, often revealing a clear direction forward or clarifying options. Such an approach to consensus was pioneered years ago by the Presbyterian Church of Aotearoa New Zealand and has been incorporated into experiments of several other denominations and church organizations.

While consensus refers to the method used in decision-making, discernment refers to the underlying spirit and style that is present. Thus, within a method of consensus, space will continually be opened and interactions encouraged that allow for deeper discernment. This may include integrated times of prayer, periods of silence, sharing in groups of just two or three, biblical reflection, storytelling, and other similar means to infuse the process of seeking consensus with the qualities of humility, intuition, and imagination.

We have seen this happen now in numerous settings, from local congregations to denominational synods to ecumenical assemblies. When a church body is ready to embark on a journey of transformational, missional change, its organizational culture will necessarily change. The focus becomes a search for God's preferred and promised future. Discovering this requires the nurture of life together that is bathed in a climate of discernment rather than debilitated by procedures of argumentation. The practices that allow a climate of discernment to grow and to flourish face their own serious difficulties and are not easily learned, in part because so much else must first be unlearned. But this is the way forward that equips a church body with the capacity to imagine and then earnestly seek the future that God has been preparing for them.

CHAPTER FOUR

Dwelling in the Word

Imagine a group of local churches from several different denominations, even some that see themselves as non-denominational churches. In the minds of a handful of their leaders, they are joining together to answer the question of God's preferred and promised future. For most of those gathered, they are there to explore ways of learning and doing mission together as local churches in the same community. Others have come to accompany friends and to grow as Christians.

The designated leader stands, a woman from the organizing group, and invites everyone to join her in prayer. She calls on the Holy Spirit to guide the work of the day, a Saturday, especially the opening time of "Dwelling in the Word of God." After the prayer, she turns to the group and says that they want to begin by dwelling in the word of God. She hands out a printed text from Scripture (Luke 10:1–12, in this case) and projects the same text on the two screens in the room so everyone can see the Scripture and, if they want, write comments on the page. She invites people to set aside the printed text and prepare to listen as a volunteer agrees to read the passage of Scripture aloud. She says that after listening to the reading, each person will be invited to find a reasonably friendly-looking stranger and "listen them into free speech" on what they heard in the reading of the Scripture. To aid their listening, each person is invited to answer one of two questions: (1) Where did your imagination get caught as the Scripture was read aloud? (2) As result of listening to this Scripture, is there a question that came to mind that you would like to ask a biblical scholar?

The Scripture is read aloud and a period of silence, a few minutes, is allowed. Then the leader invites each person to find their "reasonably friendly-looking stranger"— someone they do not know but with whom they feel safe enough to listen into free speech. This time, the leader invites the pairs to listen to the Scripture read once again before listening each other into free speech. After a few moments of silence, the pairs are told they have ten minutes to listen to each other. After ten minutes, they move to another pair and report to them what they heard from their reasonably friendly-looking stranger. After another ten minutes or so, the individuals in the foursomes are invited to report what they heard, not what they said, to the full group. The leader gathers these insights and comments on large pieces of paper that can be referred to throughout the day. Members of the group are invited to check out these notes during breaks in the day. The leader explains that they will continue to dwell in the word of God throughout the day and that anytime someone wants to invite the group to dwell in the word, they may. They can simply say, "I call for the word," or "I call for the gospel." Someone then reads the Scripture, and people listen another reasonably-friendly person into free speech. Those who choose can report back what they heard, not what they said. This becomes a regular part of the work of the day; it is always the order of the day.

This relatively organic practice, what we call Dwelling in the Word, represents the most consistently independent variable in the capacity of a local church to effectively discern God's preferred and promised future. That is to say, when a local church dwells consistently in the Scriptures in this way, a very different kind of conversation results than when they don't. Dwelling in the Word over a significant period of time opens the conversation to Christian innovation better than any other activity we have used.

Time

Time seems to be the primary factor in the success of the practice of Dwelling in the Word as part of a spiritual journey of discerning God's preferred and promised future. Beginning in the word of God, after a simple prayer asking for guidance by the Holy Spirit, sets the spiritual journey on a healthy path.

Beginnings make a massive difference. Beginnings—led by a plainspoken, low-key leader who in very few words explains the practice—establish the opening moments of an effective holding environment that is so vital to a successful spiritual journey. Make the introduction short, clear, and simple. Move to actually doing the practice as soon as possible. Reiterate that this is an exercise in *listening* to God's word in, with, and under others' hearing of God's word.

In a set of longitudinal studies of Dwelling in the Word, in a number of cultures and societies, the amount of time in the initial silence seems particularly important. Especially among the middle and upper-middle classes in English-, Dutch-, and German-speaking Europe and North America, the capacity to dwell in silence upon first hearing the scriptural passage is a high indicator of the success of the longer spiritual journey. If the gathered leadership group can dwell in silence for at least ninety seconds, the chance of long-term success goes up dramatically. In those settings where the leadership group cannot dwell in silence for at least ninety seconds, the chance of long-term success goes down. This is not a direct correlation. Significant aberrations from this general pattern exist. Like many patterns outside the norm, they tend to confirm the norm. Even in these significant aberrations, the long-term practice of Dwelling in the Word is almost always a critical part of the successful spiritual journey, as participants have reported to researchers at the end of their journeys. Some of these studies follow up with groups five or ten years after their initial spiritual journey to discern God's preferred and promised future begins, and the same patterns of capacity to take sufficient time continue years later.

Another significant temporal factor is how long the local church remains dwelling in a particular passage. We have found in longitudinal studies that dwelling in the same Scripture for a full year increases the capacity of the local church to enter the holding environment necessary for Christian innovation.

This is not to say that dwelling in the same Scripture passage does not create some kickback. It does, of course. Often local churches that complain most bitterly during the first six- to nine-month period about dwelling in the same text are the ones that complain most when we move to a new Scripture passage for the second year of the spiritual journey! Of course, other Scripture passages can play into the spiritual journey, but the holding environment is greatly enhanced by dwelling in the same passage for a year.

Amazingly, a church's sense of time either kills or gives life to the church. In so many churches in Western culture, three to five years of discernment, experimentation, learning, and reinforcing existing missional practices and establishing new ones seems like an eternity.

Too often churches refuse to make time for spiritual discernment. Some churches are so anxious and discontented that they remind me of how I (Pat) often feel when arriving late at an airport I do not know well. Once I am through security, I am tempted to head to the first plane of my preferred airline without checking where it is going. I am such a frequent flyer that I feel more at home in a plane seat than I do in many other places when I am away. Once I was in such a hurry, I actually got on the wrong plane, only to find that out when the person whose seat I was in came to rightfully claim it.

Frankly, I find many church leaders so anxious and fearful that they want to do something—anything!—to give the impression that they are making a difference. Sometimes the level of chaos they face rewards this "take charge and do something" behavior. In some situations, such take-charge behavior is warranted; however, in those circumstances when it is rewarded, it is usually still at the expense of attending to and taking the time to practice long-term spiritual discernment.

In our work, we know these pressures well, but we also know the wisdom of taking time. We have walked with each other and many other leaders as they were tempted by quick fixes while trying to capture the energy of the Holy Spirit toward God's preferred and promised future.

Rowan Williams, former archbishop of the Church of England, noted wisely that we might still be in the early church. Seldom do we experience this sense of time when encountering local-church leaders or those who care for them. More often than not, we experience the deeply disturbing sense that church leaders anticipate the death of the church but are willing neither to say it out loud nor to take the time, considerable time, to discern God's preferred and promised future. Given this sense of time, they are very likely to do many, many good things that diffuse the energies of their church into nothingness. Of course, there are those church leaders who use the sense of eternity, or the long view of church history, as a way of escaping the necessity to discern the concrete and specific vocation of God's preferred future now. Too often, we find thought leaders in the church, through their capacity to see things from a fifty-thousand-foot perspective, distancing themselves from the anxiety, discontent, pain, and fear that leaders of local churches and those who care about them cannot escape. We try in our leadership and in this book to take seriously the greater sense of time that God's promised future creates while taking very seriously the demands and pressing necessity of discerning God's preferred future in the here and now.

Space

While the sense of time, including creating time for discernment, remains the most significant factor in the spiritual journey of change, creating space is also very important. Often a key ingredient to creating the sense of time for a successful holding environment is the space the group is inhabiting. In the early stages it seems to be very important to create a space different from the usual spaces used for governing the local church or denominations as a whole.

Spaces can enhance, sometimes prevent, a sense of worshipful work. This is a very subtle but significant issue. We have both noticed that national and regional churches have shifted their governing meetings to a more worshipful and celebratory format. On the whole, this shift was very needed. However, many short-term participants experience such events to be more publicity events—celebrations designed to increase loyalty but not events where real work is done. In this book, we value celebratory worship and want all governing activities to build trust, but these events cannot be a substitute for the hard work of spiritual discernment. While certain worship can create the space and time for spiritual discernment, we find that most of these worship events do not. The concept of worshipful work has more to do with having a sense of working with the presence of God and discerning within the life of the Trinity while engaging in ordinary conversation. This is worshipful work.

Learning to create spaces that are distinct from the normal spaces for worship and governing, where the local church can enter a different sense of time, makes remarkable conversations possible. These conversations then free the group to imagine a very different sense of God's preferred future within the horizon of God's promised future.

The Dwelling in the Word session described at the beginning of this chapter gives a simple example of creating a different space. These local churches are not used to working with one another. Nor are they accustomed to this space for worship or governing. In Dwelling in the Word, three critical practices are introduced in very simple terms: (1) find a reasonably friendly-looking stranger; (2) listen the person into free speech; and (3) report what you heard, not what you said. Let's look at these three practices individually.

Find a Reasonably Friendly-Looking Stranger

One of the realities of modern public space, the space of strangers, is the fear most people have of encountering strangers. People report dreading introducing themselves or interrupting the privacy of a stranger.

Most actually fear being shamed by these encounters. In fact, shame is probably the most unattended-to dynamic in the public life of modern societies and within the public life of churches. Indeed, we believe most members of the church have agreed to the rule that religion and faith are best left in the intimate, private spaces of our lives. When this attitude is projected onto our local churches, it tends to make them "family homes" rather than the house of the Lord. Welcome is extended, indeed, but on the same terms as a welcome into our private spaces, homes, and lives. Such hospitality, while real, is not public welcome, not "the interaction of strangers through a shared set of actions."[11] Instead, both as individual Christians and as local churches, we tend to place ourselves in prisons of privacy.

For most Americans, if the government were to demand that we not imagine our faith as belonging to the company of strangers, the public space, we would rebel. We would never accept a government-imposed prison of privacy. However, the genius of the devil—we do believe this is a deal with the devil—is to convince our own conscience that it is morally superior, even morally necessary, to keep our faith and faith values private. To be polite and respectful, to support the great blessings of a culturally diverse, democratic society, we must keep private, intimate, and unspoken in public spaces those things we most value. For many, this even means not sharing these values with our own children and family members, so intimate and private is our self-made and self-maintained prison of privacy.

One of the critical obstacles to local churches realizing their true nature as missional communities is this "prison of privacy" phenomenon. The restrictiveness of these prisons becomes especially pronounced in the so-called public assemblies or conventions of our churches, where the primal nature of the church as the assembly of God, the group of citizens called out from the whole of the city to engage in political discourse for the good of the city, is forgotten, forsaken, or in many cases seen as immoral and dangerous to public life.

Now, it is perhaps already clear that the first direction of Dwelling in the Word is actually the most innovative and, in some ways, revolutionary. We deliberately use a phrase that often creates a humorous response in the group. In short, people often laugh. Humor is by far the best way to break the power of the anxiety that arises when people are asked to do something as frightening as breaking their own imprisonment. We deliver the direction in a low-key and matter-of-fact manner precisely so that individuals are more easily freed to break their own imprisonment. They smile or even laugh out loud at the tension of "finding a reasonably friendly-looking stranger."

Of course, strangers represent potential danger, and we need to practice wisdom when it comes to interacting with them. This is the primary reason we say "reasonably friendly-looking strangers." We do not encourage unwise interaction with strangers. However, it is extremely unwise to not make some progress from living solely in safe, private, intimate spaces to sharing reasonable interactions with strangers in public spaces. This is not an either-or proposition but an admonition to use wise judgment in interacting with reasonably friendly-looking strangers. Strangers though they be, we choose to risk on the basis of using an agreed-upon public ritual for engaging with them. The ritualistic nature of the task—everyone doing the same actions and practices—creates a relatively safe space and time.

Listen One Another into Free Speech

The second direction, which is also innovative, is to "listen one another into free speech." We all know what it is like to feel that anything we say will be used against us. This sort of "fault finding" listening is very common in our culture. It is even thought to be a desirable kind of listening, the assumption being that systematically doubting everything that's said and done is morally and intellectually more sophisticated than first listening with goodwill before subjecting everything to systematic doubt.

While such listening has its place, it should not be the primary way of the church, as God's public house for his creation. To be a missional church, the church must learn to listen people into free speech. To do so requires ways of making listening safer, protecting both the speaking and listening parties from harm, and starting with a hermeneutic of goodwill rather than one of critical, systematic doubt.

Learning to listen another person into free speech begins with both spiritual and physical postures. While most of us are familiar with ways of nodding our heads, asking questions, or sitting in an open rather than closed physical posture, many of us do not have similar spiritual disciplines for listening. Both are necessary and interact fruitfully. Indeed, the entire spiritual discernment process is both deeply physical and deeply spiritual. Thirty years of studying how people either do or don't create a space and time that feels safe enough for others to speak freely has taught us that physical and spiritual postures, when combined, create those safer spaces and times— holy places.

If, for example, one of the participants cannot believe they might hear the word of God by listening the other person into free speech, it lowers the chances that they will do so. Their spiritual posture toward God's presence in the other has everything to do with what they experience. Further, if one of the participants cannot present a body posture that invites the other into free speech, the other is likely to retreat back to their own safe, private, intimate space and not share their sense of God's word. Of course, different persons and cultures have very different body postures that invite free speech. In one person or culture, an open, face-to-face, eye-to-eye contact creates invitation and welcome. For another person or culture, such an open, face-to-face, eye-to-eye contact shuts down free speech. Both lose profoundly. Likewise, over time, the practice of spiritual and physical posturing for listening another into free speech frees both the listener and the speaker from their prisons of privacy. Both are freed to hear the word of God in, with, and under the other's listening. This is a tremendous power that frees a community to discern God's preferred future.

At the risk of oversimplifying, both physical and spiritual posturing are decisively obvious to persons culturally competent in their specific place. By *obvious*, we mean that anyone with cultural competence would interpret the posture of the other person without much conscious reflection. At the same time, physical and spiritual posturing are particular to each person's body and spirit.

From childhood, one is formed in these postures mostly by practices learned but never reflected upon. For example, every culture has certain rituals of greeting when encountering strangers in a public space. In my culture a certain kind of handshake is preferred, even between people well known to each other. My maternal grandma did most of the explicit teaching about hand-shakes and other rituals. She would say, "Offer a firm handshake. Don't give a person a limp hand, like a dish-rag. But don't try to prove you have the strongest hands because you never will, and it doesn't pay to start with such a silly male competition. Look the person straight in the eye so they know they can trust you." This direct style of greeting differs from that of, say, the Inupiat of Alaska, for whom direct eye contact, even among long-known members of a small fishing village, is highly restricted. Learning to know that you have been greeted and invited into conversation—by an elder addressing the group and speaking of you, rather than by face-to-face handshakes—takes some time. After twenty-seven years of interaction with Inupiat, I (Pat) still realize how often they are making the greatest effort to listen this stranger into free speech. I especially have come to be patient enough to wait for an elder to quote me or some contribution I have made as a clear indication of their listening me into free speech. Listening one another into free speech across cultural dif-ferences is difficult but extremely important.

Physical and spiritual posturing go hand in hand. With-out the spiritual posture of expecting God to speak through the other, the proper physical postures are not likely to emerge; without the physical postures being risked, the spiritual postures are not likely to emerge. It is, of course, easier to use mock physical postures than mock spiritual postures; however, we can often deceive ourselves. We could say more on this topic, but for now, it is enough to note how critical the complex but obvious practices of spiritual and physical posturing are for listening a reasonably friendly-looking stranger into free speech.

Of course, the practices of finding a reasonably friendly-looking stranger and listening them into free speech are critical but not altogether sufficient for floating a conversation. The third practice introduced by the opening directions of Dwelling in the Word, when added to the other two, makes possible the kind of conversation that can lead to corporate spiritual discernment.

Report What You Heard, Not What You Said

The test of the first two practices of finding a reasonably friendly-looking stranger and listening them into free speech is reporting back what you heard, not what you said. It is remarkably difficult, we've found, especially for educated people, including preachers, not to take the reporting phase as an opportunity to preach or to repeat what they said to the group. It is difficult, also, for people who are not used to public speaking to do this work; however, it is easier for them to report what they heard than to repeat what they said. In short, the challenges to this practice differ among personality types and backgrounds.

But as with all public practices and rituals, it simply does not help to use individual styles or personality types as excuses for avoiding learning the necessary skills, practices, and rituals for interacting with strangers without becoming their intimates. The fact that so many of our civil and public institutions are not doing this basic civic work gives no grounds for the church to retreat to the private sphere. On the contrary, in such a culture and society as ours, the local church especially becomes the chief public space for learning these basic rituals of public life. Significant research shows that, especially for marginalized populations, churches are the most likely space for children and their parents to learn such civil, public rituals for enjoying the company of strangers without becoming close friends. More than thirty years of practice of and research on Dwelling in the Word have shown how critical reporting what you heard, not what you said, can be for freeing individuals from their self-made, self-maintained prisons of privacy.

For people who seldom, if ever, have been listened to by others, much less by strangers, this simple practice is profoundly liberating. I remember watching a woman from a South African language and culture group find a reasonably friendly-looking stranger, a man from a very different language and culture group, as the person she would listen into free speech. What they both shared was a deep spiritual posture of counting on the word of God.

With great trepidation—I could see it in her physical posturing as she walked across the room to a space occupied by her Afrikaner brother—she liberated herself, her listening partner, and eventually many others in the room, making possible a shared journey of spiritual discernment in Port Elizabeth, South Africa. When the woman heard this white Afrikaner dominee (pastor), the symbol of oppression and aggression against her and her people, seek to accurately repeat what he had heard from her, time and time again, she returned the practice by reporting back what he had said. Her capacity to do so, to move beyond her sensible behavior of systematic doubt to the freedom to report his words to the group, grew from her own spiritual and physical posture joined with his in this relatively safe space and time of Dwelling in the Word. It was not the liberation of the entire society of South Africa but a powerful holy space for holy conversation. Through such simple, obvious, yet complex interactions, the reign of God comes among us.

Doing Dwelling in the Word in such a space shifts attention to the shared word of God and the shared activity of listening one another into free speech as we listen to the word of God in, with, and under others. Through this practice, we create a new place, a holy place hosted by God.

Ways to Kill It

Thirty years of experience have taught us that the legitimate questions and suspicions of well-meaning people can be used to kill the holy place that Dwelling in the Word can create. Most of these killers are on the surface quite sensible. To put it bluntly, even the best of intentions can kill the work of the Holy Spirit at certain moments and places.

One of the prominent killers of Dwelling in the Word is the concern that it is not governed by proper teaching authority. We have found this concern especially in traditional, conservative evangelical settings where the clergy and professors of Scripture have legitimate concerns that Dwelling in the Word allows anyone present to make sense of the Scriptures. Such an open-ended, untutored reading of Scripture has been the source of much mischief and even evil. Indeed, there is no end of evidence that great wrongs have been perpetrated in the name of such "democratic" interpreting of Scripture.

Teachers are needed, indeed. However, as legitimate as this concern may be, restricting the listening and interpreting of the word of God only to clergy hardly seems a sufficient solution. It seems ironic that the churches that object so strongly to the teaching office residing in bishops should find clergy or scholars more trustworthy than laypeople or nonscholars. The expositional teaching of

Scripture from evangelical pulpits is susceptible to the same pitfalls as Dwelling in the Word. The second of the two questions asked in the Dwelling in the Word process seeks to invite curiosity and seeks the wisdom of biblical scholars.

We could list numerous specific behaviors that kill the power of Dwelling in the Word, but we won't. Suffice it to say, if one begins with a hermeneutic of suspicion, one is very unlikely to reach a practical holy space for discerning God's preferred future for the local church or the systems that care about it. This is not a plea for a world of naive trust. On the contrary, it is an encouragement to wise dependence on the leadership of the Holy Spirit.

Learning to Trust the Holy Spirit

This brings us back to one of our central claims regarding how churches change: they change by the leadership of the Holy Spirit. As church leaders and theologians, we are as suspicious of this sentence as most people. And if we did not have years of experience and, of course, the witness of the Scriptures and of Christians around the world, we would likely remain suspicious and cynical. We, too, have grown up in a culture that believes the sophisticated and morally correct person is highly suspicious of any such sweeping declaration. Part of this suspicion and cynicism is merited by the charlatans and well-meaning leaders who have done much mischief in the name of the leadership of the Holy Spirit. Surely, one of the critical practices of the church is to follow the apostle John's advice: "test the spirits" (1 John 4:1). Be that as it may, it is equally and more critically innovative in our time and place to learn the practices of trusting the leadership of the Holy Spirit.

CHAPTER FIVE

Sharing the Journey

We Are Here Now

Most leaders of congregations tend to imagine their congregation to be somewhere other than where it is now. Some imagine their congregation to be somewhere in the past; when they come to church, they experience what is happening within a framework that, in fact, no longer exists, although it surely exists within their imagination. Others imagine their congregation to be significantly less than it really is. Sometimes this takes the form of imagining the local church as made up of smaller numbers than are actually active in the life of the church. Other leaders are constantly comparing the local church against some other church that exists mostly in their imaginations. Regardless of the leaders' imagined local church, in our model of how churches change, it is extremely important that leaders educate their imaginations as much as possible within the framework of where the local church really is. Please note: this is about the education of leaders' imaginations by the *here and now* rather than by *somewhere and sometime else*.

Once again, God is not where we *imagine* the local church to be; God is where and when the church *actually is*. If we are to connect our and congregations' spiritual journeys to the movement of God, we must be as true as we are able to be to where we really are. The more accurate our view, the more likely we are to experience God. A journey of spiritual discernment is far more likely to succeed if it begins where we really are rather than where we imagine ourselves to be. This, of course, requires the extremely important process of learning to *attend to* where the church is now. Seeking the truth of where we are now is both good and practical.

Congregational Discovery

We like to call this initial step "congregational discovery." We invite local-church leaders to become curious about their own church. Among leaders, there are some who are naturally curious. Some may be less so. If they are to lead in this journey of spiritual discernment, however, they will need to be lured into curiosity. Part of the fun of this journey is being opened up to what God is doing in the life of the local church and the community it serves. We find that a restrained energy tied to this curiosity about where the local church is now can sustain the long-term journey better than cheerleading or making a major production of the beginning of the journey. Keep it low-key, simple, and interesting. Let the discoveries in the journey become the excitement instead of manufacturing a spectacular show of energy. If you want leaders to stay in it for the long haul, the low-key focus during this phase of discovery pays off.

The holding environment is sustained primarily by Dwelling in the Word. Within this holding environment, the local-church leaders invite anyone and everyone who wants to participate in the journey to join. We find that both a general "you all come" and specific invitations to individuals based on their gifts and social location within the local church works best. Nothing about the spiritual journey is secret, private, or only for the right set of leaders. On the contrary, the journey is as public as possible. Transparency serves discovery and insight; it also builds trust—an essential ingredient in Christian community building. Forming Christian community around God's work in the community that the local church serves is the long-term outcome.

Inside Out and Outside In

We encourage local-church leaders to discover what is happening inside their local church and how that moves out into the lives of the broader community. We also encourage them to discover what is happening in the various publics within the community they serve. In short, going from the inside out and outside in.

Of course, several problems arise the moment you try to do this sort of discovery. First, you will want to know who counts in your discovery. And before you say, "Everyone counts," we beg you to stay real. Yes, of course, everyone counts, but it is not possible to count everyone with the same depth and breadth. Therefore, admit it from the start: some people and organizations will count more than others. Name them and get some sense of why you've assigned them a higher value, even if you honestly believe that all persons are equal.

For instance, the retired college professor of religion who has been a member of the church for thirty years and chair of the church council numerous times and whose wisdom is widely respected will have the informal power that makes him "count more" than the young deacon who joined the church four years ago and who shows up at worship only half the time. Certain people in a congregation hold, in effect, an informal but effective veto power over any major congregational decisions. They cannot be ignored, but neither can the system simply acquiesce to their influence. Rather, they should be among those intentionally invited into the process and given the freedom to respond as they wish.

Since we are seeking to discern God's preferred and promised future, other less likely individuals also "count more"—namely, those who have been excluded from the pathways of power, both in society and in the church. It requires intentional, preferential actions to see that those who typically have been on the margins of decision-making and power, because of their race, class, gender, sexual orientation, cultural background, or other factors, are welcomed into the process of discernment and discovery. That is part of how God's future is drawn into our present.

Second, you will want to know how to learn from these people and organizations. In one fairly simple formula, you will want to distinguish between those ways of discovering that give you richness and those that give you reach. Most ways of discovering through people and organizations do one or the other of these best.

Many church organizations (some local churches but especially regional and parachurch organizations) use methods designed to get reach. From these methods, which are drawn from the *quantitative* social sciences, they learn a lot of interesting information, like the demographics and psychographics of a geographic area—for example, the number of Latino/Latina or African American persons. These methods measure reach but not richness. Many times this leads to decisions for mission that ignore the considerable difference between numbers and the stories and experiences that form community.

By contrast, some church organizations use methods designed to capture richness. From these methods, which are drawn from the *qualitative* social sciences, they learn stories that can reveal deep cultural values, which could lead to new relationships and shared community action.

Ideally, church organizations should use both methods together, making possible the narrating of the numbers of people within their geographic area, and more: when the local church understands the stories and culture of the people who comprise those numbers, they can act with greater empathy in forming Christian community engaged in God's mission, right where they are.

Third, if you want the building of Christian community to be your primary outcome as you seek God's preferred future, then you'll want to invite people from within the local church and others who are not part of it to help you with discovery. The wider the community of people from whom you discover, the greater the chance you might form Christian community that is both deep and wide.

Steering Team and Listening Leaders

Congregational discovery works best with two different sets of practices: steering the process and doing the work of discovery. In very small local churches, some of the same people may need to do both of these practices. But in larger churches, it is best to distinguish the two, delegating them to two different groups.

A steering team works best when it's made up of people with different sets of gifts. The chair needs to be someone who enjoys helping a larger community do its work rather than someone who prefers to do it for them. The steering team needs someone who is comfortable with crunching numbers and who can help explain those numbers to people who find numbers dull or daunting. The team needs someone who is an influence broker within the local church and who respects and understands how things actually get done within the church and local community. Last but clearly not least, the steering team needs someone who is given to prayer and who can provide leadership in that area.

As congregational discovery begins, another group we like to call "listening leaders" needs to be organized and trained to carry out the process of discovery both "inside out" and "outside in." The individuals in this group have, as a major gift, the capacity to listen well and record accurately what they have heard. They also need, at least as a group, to know the church system well enough to identify those who participate in the diverse social relationships and activities that make up the local church. The group also needs members who know both the wider community and where their local church fits within that wider community.

We've outlined the process and steps that, in our experience, can equip congregations and wider denominational systems to discern God's preferred and promised future for them. We are calling the church to participate in God's ongoing mission in the world. That mission announces, anticipates, and welcomes God's reign breaking into our place and time, into people's lives, their communities, and the wider social order. Those "called out" by God into the body of Christ become the place that demonstrates in its shared life this new way of living and witnesses in word and deed God's intentions for the world.

The specific expressions of this are drawn not from the endless list of the world's sufferings and injustices, although those realities must always be carried in the incarnational attentiveness of the church. Rather, the discernment of God's particular calling for a particular part of Christ's body must be the guide. The poverty of children, the vulnerability of immigrants, the blight of opioid addiction, the trafficking of women—these and many other examples present a range of potential opportunities for a church's missional engagement, but it would be foolish for a church to try to tackle all of them. Likewise, the missional movement of God transforms the personal lives of individuals through a gospel encounter with saving grace and love seen in Jesus Christ. Those called out into the body of Christ call others into this new community, and together they are then sent out into a world so loved by God.

This participation in God's mission invites engagement in those movements and efforts that are part of the *polis* (the Greek word for city), or political life, of a society committed to bringing good news to the poor, freeing the captives, tending and guarding the gift of creation, and sowing the seeds of peace—all of which point to the preferred and promised future God intends for all that God has created. Participation in God's work of missional transformation includes liberating compassion, radical hospitality, personal rebirth, social justice, and global peacemaking.

But again, and remembering the counsel of Saint Augustine, the specific steps of faithfulness undertaken by a congregation or a church body are determined not by external need, which is endless, but by their cultivated discernment of calling. All local expressions of Christ's body are invited to discover the unique "short list" written by the Spirit that draws on that congregation's particular gifts and links them to specific points of engagement, creating a small tributary that eventually joins the

mighty river of God's redeeming and transforming love.
And this can begin when just two or three come together,
in the presence of Christ, to imagine God's preferred and
promised future.

Pain on the Pilgrimage

The metaphor of pilgrimage captures well the process
of how churches change. With roots centuries earlier in
Christian history, pilgrimages are intentional journeys of
faithfulness that break the routine of normal life. While
there is a destination, the very experience of moving in
that direction takes on holy significance. For pilgrims, the
journey itself is a pathway marked by "thin places" where
the accompaniment of God's presence seems noticeably
present. Further, while a distant destination is identified,
the pathway leading there is often uncertain and even
mistaken at times. Yet, even those dead ends bring their
own surprising rewards of grace.

Ancient experiences of pilgrimage are recollected in
the contemporary missional journeys of church bodies
toward God's preferred and promised future. What's important is the conviction that embarking on such a pilgrimage is essential for the spiritual life and well-being
of the group. Remaining safe at home and continuing to
be comfortably settled in secure habits and routines will

result in spiritual atrophy. A missional journey of transformational change is not an incidental expedition but an essential journey. That's why it's called a pilgrimage.

After Pat and I completed this manuscript, I (Wes) embarked on a famous pilgrimage in northern Spain, the Camino de Santiago de Compostela (Way of Saint James of Compostela). To prepare, I walked several miles each day. And I quickly developed a blister in the process. Blisters can be painful, and their effects can ripple through the whole body. A blister on the foot doesn't hurt only the foot. Because of its presence, you must change the way you walk to ease direct pressure on that point. This can impact your knees, as well as your hips. Altering the way you engage various muscles to compensate for the blister can cause you to throw out your back.

If your back is in pain, two treatments are possible. Ice can be applied. This essentially numbs the nerves, reducing and controlling the amount of pain that gets communicated to the brain and is felt; it also reduces swelling. Applying heat, on the other hand, draws blood to the point of the injury and in that way can stimulate the healing process.

All this serves as a living demonstration of what Paul meant in 1 Corinthians 12 when he described the interdependence of the human body as a metaphor for relationships in the body of Christ. Each part depends on the whole and is united to it. "If one member suffers, all suffer together" (1 Cor. 12:26). This belonging together is not an option or a matter of choice. Rather, it is a description of what is. "Now you are the body of Christ and individually members of it" (1 Cor. 12:27).

In the example of my blister, here's what is telling: the interdependence of my body was revealed through pain I experienced because I was on a pilgrimage. Had I continued my normal routine of drinking coffee in the morning with my wife, writing at my desk, attending meetings at church, and even getting on airplanes to go somewhere to speak, none of this would have come to my awareness. But because I began moving forward on a pilgrimage, the vulnerabilities of my body became apparent. Not only did the blister reverberate throughout, causing a bodily chain reaction, but also the strength or weakness of other body parts was tested. And nothing could be left behind; the body moved forward on its pilgrimage as a wounded but inspired whole.

So it is with the church. Settled in normal routines, the church can function in relative comfort even though gradual atrophy may be characterizing its life. But once it decides that transformational, missional change is essential for seeking God's intended future and it embarks on this journey, its points of pain and vulnerability will be revealed and will reverberate throughout the whole body. Moving ahead on a pilgrimage will create friction. Most pilgrims who walk the Camino de Santiago will say, "Don't think you can avoid getting blisters." The blisters are usually part of the experience, and the challenge is how you will deal with them and allow them to mend and heal even as you take the next steps forward.

There's more that can be learned from this analogy. If you go to the Camino de Santiago forum online and do a search for blisters, you'll find numerous threads with a wide range of advice. One approach is to use a product such as Compeed, which serves as a cushion over the blistered area. The problem comes if you apply this over a blister that is infected. Covering it over can actually spread the infection, causing it to grow and become more of a threat.

The first response to signs of conflict in a church body is often to try to cover over the conflict, keeping it out of sight and thereby minimizing its potential for harm. Contentious voices are, in effect, sealed off. But the result can often be to increase the toxicity of feelings among those whom the system is trying to ignore and keep silent. Those wounds become more infected and eventually burst, spilling out into the body.

Experienced pilgrims who treat blisters on wounded feet will say it's essential for them to be uncovered and exposed to the open air for periods of rest. That's part of the healing process. Again, so it is with church bodies. Wounds must be uncovered and exposed to the light of day to allow for healing. Hiding conflict and pain solves nothing. But airing these points of friction can begin to reduce the tension.

Still, the healing process can be painful. Entering into the liminal space required by a pilgrimage of missional change raises anxiety, exposes wounds, and may create conflict. Power dynamics get threatened. Traditional roles are challenged. All this can become fertile ground for disputes, animosities, and mistrust to erupt. Individuals may feel that their voices are not being heard, or that their faithful contributions to the church over a lifetime of service are not being appreciated. Some feel left behind. Others lose faith in leadership. And it's the decision to move forward on a missional pilgrimage that provokes these responses.

There's a saying originating in the Middle East that well describes these dynamics: "The dogs are barking but the caravan is moving." Countless times, in both congregational and denominational settings, we have witnessed this reality and have come to expect it. When a church body starts moving out on a missional pilgrimage, voices of alarm will suddenly be raised. You must hear and acknowledge them, openly. But you must not make the mistake of halting the caravan once it has begun its journey.

A Shared Journey

Each of the estimated 350,000 congregations in the United States tends to assume that their journey is unique. It's a symptom of how individualism so deeply infects our culture, even altering the realities of institutions that are precious to us. When we spend time listening to the journeys of congregations, it is inspiring to see when they undertake an honest effort to discover the inner realities of their composition, values, habits, fears, and aspirations. But with this, in nearly every case, comes the assumption that their congregational journey is unique and unlike any other.

Of course, that's not true. Certainly there are distinctive features in any congregational journey, and these are a joy to discover, cherish, and share. But in a post-Christendom culture, where nine out of ten congregations have an age profile that is higher than that of society at large, and where the number of white participants in churches continues to decline, the broad features of most congregations are similar. They are navigating common terrain and are confronted with shared challenges.

Our experience at every level of the church, from local congregations to global confessional and ecumenical organizations, confirms that the pilgrimage of missional transformation needs to be taken together. In working with congregations, the most fruitful results come when partnerships are established between them. It's helpful, and even essential, for congregations to understand that the life-and-death crisis they've come to face—that which compels the desire for deep, transformative change—is not theirs in isolation and need not be confronted alone.

The examples of sustained, missional, transformational change we've witnessed nearly always have involved the means for open, vulnerable, and intentional creative sharing among congregations. This can happen in a variety of ways. A small group of congregations can agree to a three-year partnership to engage in common practices of congregational discovery and community engagement, sharing their pains as well as their joys. Deep learning is almost always the result.

Often this may begin with a commitment of pastors to a small group of peers characterized by courageous honesty, trustworthy support, and mutual learning. Such pastoral networks, providing safe places for sharing their personal and congregational journeys, reflects one of the main features (identified earlier by Craig Dykstra of the Lilly Endowment) that is needed for pastors to thrive and for their congregations to flourish in a context of tension and required change. In some programs, those networks then get extended to other congregational leaders, who are brought together in ongoing experiences of sharing, learning, and growth, which form critical links in the transformational process of their local churches.

All this makes sense, biblically, theologically, and from the standpoint of research. The body of Christ is designed, intended, and empowered by the same Spirit to exist interdependently. Such mutual belonging, even in the midst of differences, is the evident pattern enshrined in the foundational prayer of Jesus in John 17, explicated in Paul's epistles and ministry, and evidenced in the story of the church's emergence in Acts. Our contemporary tendency to retreat into protective shells of congregational autonomy not only is disobedient to uncompromising biblical admonitions but also deprives congregations of the shared wisdom, learning, and spiritual enrichment that are likely to be essential in any process of transformational change.

The diversity of congregations contributes to this enrichment and becomes a further source of mutual empowerment. The differences of theology, polity, and worship style between Pentecostal, Orthodox, Catholic, evangelical, and mainline Protestant congregations do not get reconciled, as if that were the goal. The gift of a fundamental unity in Christ is received rather than created. With that conviction, diversities become mutually enriching, reminding us that the Holy Spirit seems most present and powerful when the full diversity of Christ's body is received and celebrated. What makes this ever more possible is a shared discernment about the place of all congregations within the culture—namely, that from each of our distinctive backgrounds, we walk together in a common pilgrimage seeking the missional transformation of our presence and witness in society. We taste a unity not merely as God's gift through our mutual belonging to Christ but experienced also through our common participation in God's ongoing mission in the world.

This shared missional pilgrimage finds expression both locally and globally. The past twenty-five years have seen new initiatives that are restructuring the ecumenical architecture and guiding efforts toward broadening and deepening the search for fuller expressions of Christian unity. The ongoing work of the National Council of Churches of Christ in the USA, which has restructured and revived itself, is now also accompanied by Christian Churches Together in the USA. CCT has provided the first opportunity for the United States Conference of Catholic Bishops to participate as a full member of an ecumenical organization and has also built new bridges of cooperation with some evangelical and Pentecostal denominations previously detached from such engagement.

Globally, the World Council of Churches is a well-developed institution, recently celebrating seventy years of its ecumenical witness. More recently, the Global Christian Forum has emerged as a new ecumenical space welcoming the Vatican, the Pentecostal World Fellowship, the World Evangelical Alliance, the World Council of Churches, and other global Christian bodies into a formal and public engagement with one another for the first time in ecumenical history.

While significant on many levels, these hopeful signs set a climate for denominations and global church bodies to walk together on a common pilgrimage rather than to persist in going down separate and isolated pathways. With intention, after its General Assembly in Busan in 2013, the World Council of Churches framed all its programmatic efforts as a "pilgrimage of justice and peace." This emerging ecumenical architecture provides the opportunity and the encouragement for church bodies to share more freely with one another in their journeys of missional transformation.

Just as congregations cannot effectively engage in a search for God's preferred and promised future by remaining in their prideful isolation from others, neither can denominations. Throughout various denominational headquarters, leaders are earnestly (and sometimes frantically) seeking fresh methods and strategies for their future in ways similar to that pictured in the fictional but all-too-real description of the Reverend Sheldon Keating in the introduction to this book. Yet, many do so in isolation from the stories and journeys of other denominations. Ecumenical activities, when embraced, lead to the discovery of a common voice of social witness or common ground in the face of theological differences. But denominations should go further and learn to embrace those ecumenical relationships as a vehicle of God's Spirit to support and nurture their own missional transformation of change.

Some experiences offer a window into what those possibilities could look like. In the 1990s a small group of denominational leaders and chief executives—with a variety of titles like presiding bishop, president and general minister, stated clerk, general secretary, general superintendent, and others—decided to try meeting together for a year-end, off-the-record retreat. Their site was the College of Preachers on the grounds of Washington National Cathedral. Their format was simple but radical in its own way. The first afternoon and evening, each leader would share confidentially what their year had been like—its pains, joys, surprises, and disappointments. Then they all would enter into twenty-four hours of silence, committed to prayer and reflection, including praying for one another. Finally, they would conclude by sharing what came out of that silence and by reflecting on the year ahead.

About a dozen or so joined. For most, this became a precious, pivotal time marking the year's end. They easily discovered the common points in their journeys. All recognized that, in one way or another, their denominations were facing life-and-death issues. All knew that deep change was essential. All earnestly desired to find God's preferred and promised future, regardless of how they might theologically explain and express this. And in their honesty, and in the midst of their well-developed plans, most shared doubts about how desired change would actually come about. There were successes and joys to celebrate but also wounds and pain to share.

This was only forty-eight hours in a long year. Yet it decisively interrupted their normal schedule and style of doing business. It became a liminal time for each of them individually and for the group as a whole. Moments of fresh discernment emerged, seeds that for some would take root and blossom in initiatives of institutional transformation. None of this would have happened if they had not become committed to sharing their journeys with one another.

Here's an analogy. Rev. Kyle Small, a seminary professor and veteran pilgrim of the Camino de Santiago, shares that, in his experience, one of the most precious and memorable times of the journey came in the evening, at the *albergues* or pilgrim hostels. There, pilgrims gathered together and often shared about their blisters. They ministered to one another with ways to ease the pain and promote healing. And then they encouraged one another to start again the next morning, walking together in the new day of their common pilgrimage.

Those year-end retreats shared by the heads of US denominations were like that. By being willing to share their journeys, they found balm for their wounds and discovered strength for the next step in a common pilgrimage. At every level of the church, from the small conference room by a pastor's study in Waterloo, Iowa, to the assembly hall of the WCC in Geneva, we must embrace the truth that our desire to seek God's preferred and promised future—for our church and for the world—can never be discovered in isolation. Our shared pilgrimage is, in fact, the gift of God's Spirit, through whom we can provide healing, hope, wisdom, and courage to one another in the next steps of our shared pilgrimage toward missional transformation.

CHAPTER SIX

Being Transformed:
Practices for Missional Change

Churches change. It is inevitable. The life of the church is within an ever-rolling stream. The forces of that stream create changes in the church and in the world it serves.

We live in a time of deep, overpowering, rapid, discontinuous change. Indeed, we cannot even successfully name all the change, much less its outcomes. We experience this ever-rolling stream as white water, the roils of spring runoff in the mountains of the West—high, incredibly fast, dirty, murky, dangerous, life-threatening. This experience of contemporary change drives the church in all its types, whether small groups, independent free churches, or highly organized churches. We find many expressions of the church in considerable disarray trying desperately to control that change. Or at least trying to respond faithfully and effectively to some of the immediate forces of that change on and in our churches. Like in white-water rafting, we seek to meet the immediate challenges of rocks, eddies, and falls—unseen and unknown. Our primary purpose is to survive the immediate challenge and make it to the next one.

We see abundant examples of two tragic responses to this inevitable river-rapids-like change. These two tragic responses form a spectrum of ways we seek to control change, or at least the processes for responding to change. First, and seldom purely attempted, we seek to not change. We deeply value what has been handed down to us. We don't want to lose it in the ever-flowing stream. We recognize the value and virtue of deep roots but fail to do the very hard work of finding the minimal identity of those roots. Instead we hang on to everything, in effect declaring that all the practices that have successfully brought us to this place must be preserved, protected, secured. Who can know which one will prove successful in the coming white-water challenges! We see the church as the one place in the white water where change does not happen, or at least where change should not be seen. All too often such churches do not take up the very difficult task of identifying those life-giving practices that faithfully and effectively keep the raft on a relatively safe course.

The other extreme response is to seek to control by changing everything. Of course, this is seldom done, any more than controlling by seeking never to change. Such churches respond, quite willy-nilly, to every perceived challenge. With a genuine desire to respond to the many good things to love and to do, such churches attempt to do them all. In the face of this tragic pole, we have taken seriously Saint Augustine's recognition that when we seek to love all the good that God gives us, we end up more often than not in "disorderly love"—that is, placing our affection and desire on things that are not in God's order for us. In our desire to do all good things simply because they are good, we end up, again and again, in disorderly love. Such disordered love Augustine calls sin. And so it is. We find few churches consciously seeking to love evil—that is, to do bad things—but we find most churches trying to love all good equally, and to do all good things simply because they are good things to do. Augustine instead advises us to create short lists, with clear priorities, based on one desire: seeking first the kingdom of God—the power, will, space, and time of God. Because such seeking is primarily about desire, it must address those deep places where our desires live and breathe, those places of the spirit.

We have proposed a relatively simple process of discernment for seeking God's preferred and promised future. Rather than speak of such discernment as a lofty aspiration, we have tried to stay with simple, concrete, embodied practices. They are very down-to-earth.

As you have seen, these down-to-earth spiritual practices are designed to shape our desire to seek God's preferred and promised future and have both deeply personal and deeply public dimensions. We have found one Scripture text very helpful in reflecting on both dimensions and how they interact with each other. Ironically, the text comes from Paul's letter to the Philippians, thought to be one of the few New Testament letters addressed to a local church that is *not* conflicted.

Paul begins by commending a life worthy of the gospel. The phrase he uses in this case is "only let your *politeusthe*" be worthy of the gospel (Phil. 1:27). Even to an English speaker, this term reveals much upon patient observation. The word *polite* is clearly present, carrying with it the association of courtesy; it is a derivative of the common Greek word for city, *polis*, as in Indiana*polis* or Minnea*polis*. The term *politeusthe* would be recognized by Paul's audience as referring to what a young man would begin to do when he became a citizen of the city: he would begin to engage in a public discourse with other citizens on behalf of the good of the city.

This act of public discourse took place in a special group, an *ecclesia*. The ecclesia, in common city-state discourse, was the group called out from the general population of a city to carry out the city's business. Paul borrowed this political term to name the church. The church was the *ecclesia tou theou*, the assembly of God. It follows, then, that Paul's advice to the Philippians pertains to how they were to conduct their political engagement on behalf of the city.

As is typical of Paul, he is blunt: they are to share "the same mind that was in Christ," to "stand firm in one spirit, with one mind striving side by side for the faith of the gospel." And what is that "one spirit" and "one mind"? Paul is equally clear: it is not a set of doctrines, ideas, thoughts, or feelings but a set of practices, literally things Jesus did.

Jesus had equality with God but did not exploit it. Again, using political experience, imagine those who have full access to the president of the United States not using such access to influence the president's policies, appointments, or other actions for their own benefit. Imagine having such intimacy as Jesus had with God, being one with the Father and the Holy Spirit, and not exploiting that intimate relationship. In stark contrast to our political experience, Jesus emptied himself of such power and influence, such intimate equality with God. And not just emptied himself but emptied himself into "the form of a servant." Being found in human form, he became fully vulnerable to the powers and principalities of this world. He became obedient to the will of humans for their sake, not his own.

In Philippians Paul follows a very common argument of the ancient Greco-Roman world—an argument about what makes a civilization possible. How could a city (*civitas* in Latin) organize itself? The theory went that without slaves, civilization was not possible. If there were to be citizens able to *politeusthe*—engage in political discourse for the good of the city as members of the ecclesia—someone needed to be making the household possible. Someone needed to carry on the labor of farm and home so that the citizens could govern on behalf of the whole. Those who carried on while the citizens carried out the governance of the city were women, slaves, and children. If you are uncomfortable with this line of argument, you are not alone. It is truly scandalous. And it gets worse.

Paul offers a Christian theory of democracy. For John Locke and Thomas Jefferson, the equality of the *demos* ("people" in Greek) was based on each person being their own king or queen—that is, subject to no one but themselves and, of course, the law. Paul, in contrast, says to the Philippians: Follow Jesus's example. First be slaves, not masters or mistresses. Have the same mind (the practices) that was in Christ—a slave who sought to serve, not to be served.

As if that were not discomforting enough, Paul goes on to say that Jesus was obedient to the laws of humanity to the point of death, even death on a cross. Citizens in the Greco-Roman world could not be crucified in most circumstances, but slaves could. Indeed, at the will (and often whim) of their master or mistress, they could be put to death through this vile, humiliating, excruciatingly painful form of execution. This was precisely the form of execution Jesus endured, and that action of his is what frees us to be citizens in the assembly of God. In Paul's theory of democracy, we are first slaves to one another. This mutual self-emptying, this seeking the good of the other (even the other who is not a part of the assembly), is how we live out our shared citizenship in the kingdom of God.

We find this proposal for Christian political discourse—life on behalf of the city and of the world God so loves—discomforting, daunting, and indeed offensive and frightening. On its surface it is seemingly impossible, designed to frustrate and lead to failure. Without presuming 100 percent success, we have proposed a model of participating in the change into which God invites the church, and it consists simply of following Jesus's example of servanthood, which we have found to be amazingly practical. When leaders of public conversation within the church empty themselves of their own desires and seek to free others into speech, the dynamics of discernment and decision-making change, as does the capacity of the church to change. For this posture to become instinctive, it helps to practice. Practice does not make perfect, but it often makes for improvement over time.

Six Holy Practices for Missional Change

Over the past thirty years we both have done a great deal of experimenting with ways of freeing churches to experience missional change. We have found that most practices in churches are there for the good reason that at one time or another in the past, they were successful in bringing vitality and faithfulness to the church. The frustrating part of the work we are inviting you to is precisely the struggle with practices that once worked and proved productive but that are no longer doing so. We do not want to throw out all a church's traditions, because we are both convinced that tradition represents the living faith of the dead. Indeed, we seek to find the usable past for a faithful future. The practices we have offered do just that.

In addition to having clear ties to past practices, these practices are organic. They can be learned and done by most without much explanation. In fact, we recommend you "just do them" rather than give a long explanation beforehand. After you have tried them out a few times, questions will arise. Indeed, some rebellion usually arises, and this becomes the occasion for the critical disruptive experience necessary for the practices to work both personally and communally. In short, they are traditional, organic, and disruptive practices.

1. Dwelling in the Word

As already explained, the primal practice, or holy habit, that we call Dwelling in the Word has deep roots in the Christian tradition. Our proposed model follows from the *lectio divina* tradition, with Reformation precedents as well.

Be that as it may, we have also found instances in which Dwelling in the Word creates significant pushback. We have especially found significant frustration and anger with dwelling in the same text of Scripture for a year's time among Protestants who are used to viewing the Bible as a text to study and mine for nuggets of knowledge and wisdom. In both liberal and conservative Protestantism, the dominant pattern is of the Bible as sacred object and the Christian as active subject who uses this object to learn through disciplined study. Dwelling in the Word clearly upsets that dynamic by allowing the Scriptures to rule the imagination and leave the Christian dependent on the movement of the Spirit over time and through others. We find that Dwelling in the Word creates both conflict and spiritual insight.

One of the key dynamics in Dwelling in the Word takes shape in the practice of seeking out a reasonably friendly-looking stranger and listening them into free speech. We introduce this practice as if it is the easiest and most natural thing to do. We know, however, from research and experience that it is far from easy or natural for most people to seek out a stranger and listen them into free speech. We deliberately use the phrase "a reasonably friendly-looking stranger," hoping the somewhat high level of anxiety that surrounds this practice for most people gets diffused through the humor of the expression. Of course, we know many will not seek out a true stranger the first time they engage in Dwelling in the Word. Over time, however, more and more individuals take the plunge as they see how doable it is.

Listening a reasonably friendly-looking stranger into free speech is the beginning of Dwelling in the Word. The skill of sitting with a reasonably friendly-looking stranger at church makes doing the same in many other public places easier. After all, in public is where strangers engage in shared action. Once the practice becomes familiar, it transposes quite easily into other public locations.

2. Hospitality

Throughout its history, humanity has been thoroughly nomadic, with major portions of the species moving from place to place. Clearly one of the central practices necessary for thriving in nomadic existence is hospitality.

Although it is possible to read the Holy Scriptures ignoring this theme of hospitality, we find the theme deeply wise and practical for allowing missional change within a church. Hospitality within the scriptural tradition has two poles: being hosted and hosting. We find that most churches tend to put the emphasis on hosting. While this is a critical dynamic in the practice of hospitality, the danger of putting the emphasis on hosting is that it allows the church, whether local or global, to remain in control of the practice. For biblical hospitality, however, the emphasis needs to be on the church's capacity *to be hosted*. Learning to be hosted and experiencing hospitality from this pole of the practice—being in the position of strangers and recipients rather than always hosts and providers—frees churches to become more porous on their boundaries and more centered on their core values, their tradition.

3. Announcing the Reign of God

We have found "announcing the reign of God" to be, in many settings, the most difficult, indeed, almost untouchable practice. In mainline churches, many would reduce this practice to performing some "good and righteous act" but avoid the irreducible need to announce, to speak, to say, to introduce another to the reign of God. Most of the time, we find that church members deeply fear exercises that ask them to think about their everyday lives in terms of what God is up to there. Although few would deny that God is up to something in their lives, they fear speculating about what that activity might look like.

Needless to say, it will be difficult for anyone to share their own experience of God's movement in their life in a communal discernment process if everyone is filled with fear of even giving it a go. While certainly such discernment often takes place in reflection back over time, Christians nevertheless live by their sense of God's faithfulness not only in the past but now and into the future. They are free to risk making a judgment and announcing their sense of the space, time, and power of God in their lives.

Many will argue against such moments of discernment and in humility avoid making any claims regarding what God might be up to in the communities in which they live. We often remind them that the promise of the Holy Spirit by our Lord is to guide the church in faith, hope, and love. Of course, the church will get it wrong. Infallibility belongs to God alone; however, the church depends on and lives out of the future promise of God's mercy. If the church does not fail, get it wrong, or sin, God has no need of being merciful. Avoiding the risk of announcing the reign of God on the grounds that we might get it wrong misses the point altogether. Of course we get it wrong! Otherwise, we would not need God's mercy or experience the power of God's reconciling love within Christian community. We have this ministry of reconciliation precisely to empower and encourage us to risk on such communal discernment.

4. Public/Corporate Spiritual Discernment

Gathering as a company of strangers (some stranger than others!), as the ecclesia, exercising corporate spiritual discernment, is a central characteristic of the church. We are the ones called out of the city to be the assembly of God, to engage in discernment for the good of the city and the world. Learning to exercise this calling and risking the tough political work follows from being the assembly of God.

If the church, whether local or global, is to order its love in accordance to God's preferred and promised future, corporate spiritual discernment needs to happen. Of course, there is tremendous chaos and conflict in the midst of such discernment. Yes, people will get hurt and the church will fail. Once again, this follows from the fact that God is merciful and gives to us the ministry of reconciliation. This is the center of the church's missional identity.

5. Focusing on Mission

Precisely *in* the rather chaotic and conflict-ridden struggle to discern God's preferred and promised future is the emancipation of the church. Once a local church, for example, learns to move beyond its private interests and to be open to God's preferred and promised future, it becomes much easier for that church to focus on the mission into which God invites it. Such a church learns the practice of creating very short lists. Then, with a shared sense of God's preferred future, the church holds itself accountable to the steps, milestones, and especially the "big rocks" it believes are best for walking into God's preferred future. The big rocks are the essential, major, primary pieces of a plan. Smaller rocks become important only after the big rocks are put into place. The spiritual discipline of mission can become habit forming. When it does, it is truly miraculous. We have seen many such miracles. Remember this: a missional church is one which centers its life and identity on its commitment to participate in God's ongoing mission in the world.

6. Readiness

We have consistently found certain characteristics of readiness for this work. First, *a central desire to do what God desires*. It is not enough to be aware that the church is fighting for its survival. Adaptive denial must be recognized, and those who wish to experience missional change must desire to set it aside. Sadly, it is commonplace for churches, like all systems, to confuse a desire to do what God desires with changes that only serve to continue the denial of the underlying crisis. For example, noting that the median age of a church is going up and then starting youth programs is adaptive denial; it does something different, but it does not address the deep cultural crisis. Second, *a focus on providing places, times, and spaces where people feel free to explore and innovate rather than focusing on decision-making processes*. Third, *communal discernment allowing for spiritual experimentation and play that lays aside parliamentary decision-making processes*. Fourth, *a deep dwelling within the biblical story* with significant periods of time spent dwelling in one text to such a point that it shapes a communally shared sense of God's movement in the world. Fifth, *a willingness to engage this work ecumenically*, across divisions and different Christian communities—a willingness that is worth the extra effort both locally and globally.

Conclusion

In the end, the readiness for transformative, missional change is a mystery. We know the practices that can help. These prepare the ground. But how and when they yield new growth, rooted deeply, still comes as a surprise, nurtured by the pervasive but unexpected presence of God's grace.

This much we do know: the transformative, missional change so deeply needed by the church in our time, both local and global, will not come through quick fixes, catchy slogans, inspiring weekend speakers, and neat formulas wrapped in consulting fees. The change the church needs, which we have witnessed occurring in specific congregations, wider assemblies, and denominational governing bodies, comes slowly and patiently. It takes time, because culture is being changed. It takes practice, because new habits are being formed. And it takes trust, because a familiar, comfortable past must be left behind before the future can be fully discerned. But this is, after all, the nature of Christian faith.

Questions for Discussion

Introduction

1. The introduction relates the stories of Helen and Chris (pp. 1–7). What resonated with your own experience as you read their stories? What could you relate to? Were there things that puzzled you or seemed surprising?

2. The introduction also discusses the findings of the Institute for Religion Research's comprehensive study of US congregations in 2015 (pp. 8–10). The Hartford study asked people about a number of things, two of which turned out to have a notable connection: (1) a church's attitude toward and ability to change and (2) the reported "vitality" of the church.

- What has been your church's experience with change? How open has the church been to change? When the church has been willing to change, has there been the capacity or ability to do so? While change is always disturbing and disruptive to some extent, has change been generally experienced as positive or negative?

- What do you think are the marks or indicators of vitality for a church? What does "vitality" mean and what does it look like?

3. Think of a time when your church, or another church you know of, has tried to change. If it was not able to change, why do you think it didn't work? If it was able to change, what made that possible?

Chapter One: What Needs to Change, and How?

Scripture forms our imaginations as Christians. It gives shape to our understanding of who we are, who God is, and the character of our relationships with God, the world, and each other. One of the most formative stories for Christians (and also for Jews) is the story of Abraham as the ancestor of the faith and archetype of a follower of God. The church is being called by God into a new era. Read the story of God's initial call to Abram (whose name will be changed to Abraham) in Genesis 12:1–4.

1. What resonates with you in Abram's call here? What do you think this says to the larger church about God's call in our time?

2. Think back to the story of the church leaders from the beginning of the chapter. Note particularly the three attitudes listed on p. 27. What parallels do you see with the call of Abram?

3. Notice particularly the end of Genesis 12:3: God sends Abram into the unknown for a reason—that "in you all the families of the earth shall be blessed." Recall the characteristics of the missional church listed on p. 30, particularly numbers 1 and 2. How might the sending of Abram connect to the missional church?

4. Abram experiences fear and doubt on his journey, even attempting to pass off Sarai (Sarah) as his sister to avoid conflict, but God renews God's promise and swears on God's own life to bring about that which is promised (Genesis 15:18). So in the journey of missional transformation there will surely be moments of failure and doubt (pp. 33-34).

- How does your church handle failure? Is there sufficient trust in God's promise of future blessing to allow the congregation to handle delay or less-than-complete success?
- What about doubt and questions? How are people allowed to voice fear, disappointment, and questions about God's activity?
- How might a shift in attitude open up space for transformation and renewal?

Chapter Two: Making Space

The people of Israel spent forty years in the desert on their way from Egypt to the Promised Land. The length of the journey was determined not so much by the miles to travel as by the transformational change they needed to undergo. The slaves who left Egypt were not the people who would be able to move into the Promised Land. This time in the desert is what the chapter describes as "liminal space" (p. 46), that threshold experience in which we no longer inhabit the familiar but have not yet entered God's preferred and promised future.

1. Recall the conversation Wes had on a bus ride with Nelus Niemandt, a delegate from the Dutch Reformed Church of South Africa. Nelus spoke of the deep need to *disrupt* the normal functioning of church systems "if deep change were ever to have any chance of taking root" (p. 40). When have you found this to be true in your life or ministry? Some people like to disrupt, and others prefer to make change incrementally and keep things on an even keel. Which way do you lean? Why is that important to you? What value might there be in encouraging the other way?

2. In the Exodus story, God disrupts Israel's life by leading them out of slavery. Even though they had been complaining about their hardships when they were slaves,

once they got to the desert they longed to go back to what was familiar (Exodus 16). Does this resonate with your experiences? Have there been times when you longed for a change, only to discover that change itself was difficult—so difficult that you wished you could go back? On the other hand, have there been times when your life has been disrupted in ways you didn't like, but in retrospect it seems like it might have been the hand of God? Has this been the case in the history of your church or a church you know?

3. Disruption is not an end in itself. The chapter suggests that it is valuable in making space for something new to emerge (p. 42). During their liminal time in the desert, the people of Israel had much to learn about trusting God and living as God's people. Have there been liminal times in your life when you sensed that God was working to bring something new, even though you may have felt "in the wilderness"? What helped you in those times? Do you see any similarities to the spiritual resources Israel had in their time in the wilderness?

4. The chapter discusses the New Testament's two words for time: *chronos* and *kairos* (p. 56). There was once a pastor who stopped calling the inevitable interruptions in his day "interruptions" and began calling them "God appointments." Can you think of disruptive "God appointments" in your life? How might church look different if we ex-

pected—and made space for—God's interruptions in our typical pattern of "doing church"? How might you begin to create "sacred space" for God's disruptive movement?

Chapter Three: Nurturing a Climate of Discernment

1. A church's culture includes many expectations and norms, sometimes made explicit in writing or otherwise, but oftentimes unspoken or assumed, yet nevertheless used as a measuring stick and communicated and enforced in various ways. Identify some of the expectations—both of members and clergy—that make up the culture of your church. Here are some things to consider and discuss:

- What are the expectations around things like frequency of worship attendance, personal spiritual practices, education, service within and beyond the congregation?
- What are the norms of interaction, relationship, and support? Are folks expected to be demonstrative/affectionate with one another? To spend time together outside of "official church time"? How are members and clergy expected to support and care for members in times of crisis, illness, or death?
- What "lifestyle expectations" operate in your congregation? What are the expectations of political or so-

cial action or advocacy—or the expectation that such things are kept private? What are the implicit or explicit expectations regarding family and relationships and roles in personal life for members and clergy?

- How is hospitality extended to visitors? How are people welcomed? What is the process for people to explore faith and a growing Christian identity?
- What is your church's relationship to its surrounding community? To the larger denomination or religious tradition or affiliation? To the other churches or houses of worship in your town, city, or neighborhood?
- What are other aspects of your church's culture?
- What is your church's culture for navigating situations where people do not meet these expectations or transgress these norms?

2. Nurturing a climate of spiritual discernment in decision-making is one of the key elements impacting a church's capacity for transformation.

- How are decisions made in your church? What are the formal and (maybe more importantly) informal procedures for decision-making and bringing about change in the congregation?
- Who has influence, not only on what is decided, but also on what is proposed for consideration before getting to the point of discussion and decision?

- What role do the clergy play currently? Is this the role they have typically played or has that changed either with time or with the people involved?

3. Discuss the nature and strengths of spiritual discernment.
   - What is spiritual discernment?
   - What are its aspects or qualities?
   - How is it different from the usual process of decision-making?
   - What are the strengths of this process?

4. One of the important ways spiritual discernment brings about missional transformation in a church's culture is by shaping people's imaginings. By *imaginings* we do not mean mere fantasy, things that exist in our minds but are not real or practical. Rather, we mean that the pictures we have in mind about how things are, or how they should be, will have a significant impact on what we do and what we think God is doing and can do among and through us.
   - What are some of the ways we cultivate a picture of what we believe God is up to and of what God is calling us to be?
   - What practices of your church are directed toward shaping your imaginings about God's activity in the world in order to recognize it when it is happening and move toward it?

Chapter Four: Dwelling in the Word

1. What are the typical ways of interacting with Scripture in your church? What are the purposes or desired outcomes of these various ways?

2. Give Dwelling in the Word a try! Below is the text that we have dwelt in for many years, along with brief instructions for how to practice Dwelling.

> After this the Lord appointed seventy others and sent them on ahead of him in pairs to every town and place where he himself intended to go. He said to them, "The harvest is plentiful, but the laborers are few; therefore ask the Lord of the harvest to send out laborers into his harvest. Go on your way. See, I am sending you out like lambs into the midst of wolves. Carry no purse, no bag, no sandals; and greet no one on the road. Whatever house you enter, first say, 'Peace to this house!' And if anyone is there who shares in peace, your peace will rest on that person; but if not, it will return to you. Remain in the same house, eating and drinking whatever they provide, for the laborer deserves to be paid. Do not move about from house to house. Whenever you enter a town and its people welcome you, eat what is set before you; cure the sick who are there, and say to them, 'The kingdom of God has come near to you.' But whenever you enter a town and they do not welcome

you, go out into its streets and say, 'Even the dust of your town that clings to our feet, we wipe off in protest against you. Yet know this: the kingdom of God has come near.' I tell you, on that day it will be more tolerable for Sodom than for that town." (Luke 10:1–12 NRSV)

Instructions for Dwelling in the Word

(1) Pray and invite the Holy Spirit to open our ears, hearts, and minds.
(2) Listen to the passage of Scripture read out loud. Notice where your attention is drawn and your imagination caught—a verse, phrase, or single word.
(3) Remain in silence for a minute or two, staying with the place in the passage that stood out for you.
(4) Find a person in the group whom you might call "a reasonably friendly-looking stranger."
(5) Listen to that person as he or she says what they heard in the passage. They may mention something they'd never heard before, something odd or something comforting, or something about which they'd like to ask a Bible scholar. (Listen carefully without commenting.)
(6) After each has listened to the other, report to the rest of the group what your partner has said, not what you yourself said. (You may take notes to help you focus

and remember.) (In a large group, you should introduce your partner by name to the group. Each should take their turn when they are ready to speak.)

(7) If there is time, you can develop a conversation from the themes arising in the whole group around what God is saying to us today.

3. After you have done your Dwelling, answer these questions:

- What did you like about this? What was easy? What was positive?
- What was challenging? What did not seem to work well or felt difficult?

(We encourage you to continue to practice this habit in the future. It tends to bear more fruit the longer and more consistently it is practiced.)

Chapter Five: Sharing the Journey

The story of Jacob at Bethel, in Genesis 28:10–22, has some interesting parallels to the journey described in this chapter.

1. The chapter asserts that "God is not where we *imagine* the local church to be; God is where and when the church *actually is*" (p. 100). In Genesis 28, Jacob has fled

his home because he is afraid that his brother, Esau, will harm him. Jacob believes he has not only left his family but left God and God's promise behind as well. Yet during the night, in this liminal wilderness place, he has a vision of heavenly beings coming and going and hears the voice of God promising to be with him and to bless him along the way.

- When have you had an experience of discovering God in a place and time that you did not expect?

- What are your thoughts and feelings as you contemplate looking for God in the *present* circumstances of your life?

- How would looking for signs of God's activity and presence be different from a typical strategic planning process?

2. In Jacob's dream, God promises to bless Jacob and bring him back to this land. Jacob's response in the morning (paraphrased) is this: "If this works out and you do actually bless me, God, then you shall be my God." The chapter proposes that "part of the fun of this journey is being opened up to what God is doing in the life of the local church and the community it serves. . . . Let the discoveries in the journey become the excitement" (pp. 100–101).

- Many times, strategic planning tries to identify where we should go or where we would like to go. The process of spiritual discernment asks, "Where do we see or discern God moving and active?" How do you respond to that form of the question? In what ways is it confusing? Exciting? Scary?

· How would you react if you sensed that God was leading your church into a future that looked different from the past? What might God be doing in the present (right now) to open up that future?

3. In Jacob's dream, God also promises to bless Jacob and his family and, through them, all the families of the earth. We see that God's promise and mission extend to the *entire world*. The chapter explains: "This participation in God's mission invites engagement in those movements and efforts that are part of the *polis* . . . which point to the preferred and promised future God intends for all that God has created" (p. 107).

· What does the phrase "Blessed to be a blessing" mean to you? How might the welfare of your church be connected to the welfare of your community in God's mission?

· In what ways do you see God at work in your *polis* to bring about blessing? Does the church partner with that work? If so, in what ways?

4. Jacob is "on the run," in fear for his life, when he encounters God. At Bethel he discovers that God is still at work even in what is a painful and frightening time. Those

on the journey of seeking God's promised future may well share the same advice as the pilgrims along the Camino de Santiago, "Don't think you can avoid getting blisters" (p. 110). In other words, you will likely get sore and frustrated. Admit it, accept it, deal with it, and move along.

- How do you typically deal with discomfort and frustration in a journey or process of change? How might your ways of dealing with it change if you believe God is leading?
- How does your congregation deal with discomfort, frustration, and pain?
- In what ways might talking about the discomfort and frustration help? In what ways might it hurt?

Chapter 6: Being Transformed:
Practices for Missional Change

1. When you personally are going through difficult times, what are some of the habits or practices that have sustained and guided you? What did you get from those practices?

2. The chapter lists six practices or "holy habits" that have been found to be fruitful for the transformation of congregations (pp. 127–35). With your group, discuss them. Explain them as best you can (perhaps writing down a

brief description). Share questions you have about what the practices actually are (what is done in each) and try to understand them better by looking back at the chapter. What good things come about from developing these practices in a congregation?

3. Which of these transformative practices do you think your congregation could begin to engage in? Where in your church's life might this happen?

4. What are your hopes for your congregation's transformation? What is your mental picture of your congregation transformed? How could that change begin, based on what you have learned here?

Notes

1. The expression "God's preferred and promised future" is explicated in further detail later in this book. For now, it is shorthand for distinguishing the ultimate promised future of God that we have already in the life and fate of Jesus of Nazareth, the Christ, and the in-between, penultimate time before the completion of the new creation in Christ. Between now and the full realization of the new creation—that is, God's promised future in Christ—Christians seek to live out God's preferred future.

2. Darrell L. Guder, ed., *Missional Church: A Vision for the Sending of the Church in North America* (Grand Rapids: Eerdmans, 1998).

3. Craig Van Gelder and Dwight J. Zscheile, *The Missional Church in Perspective: Mapping Trends and Shaping the Conversation*, The Missional Network (Grand Rapids: Baker, 2011), 4 (Kindle edition).

4. J. Barentsen, S. van den Heuvel, and P. Lin, eds., *The End of Leadership? Leadership and Authority at Crossroads* (Leuven: Peeters, 2017).

5. Barentsen et al., *The End of Leadership?*, 55.

6. Richard Rohr, "Liminal Space," Center for Action and

Contemplation, July 7, 2016, https://cac.org/liminal-space-2016
-07-07/.

7. Richard Pascale, Mark Millemann, and Linda Gioja,
"Changing the Way We Change," *Harvard Business Review*, No-
vember–December 1997, https://hbr.org/1997/11/changing-the
-way-we-change.

8. Unless otherwise stated, all Scripture quotations in this
book are taken from the English Standard Version.

9. Charles M. Olsen, *Transforming Church Boards into Communities of Spiritual Leaders* (Herndon, VA: Alban Institute, 1995).

10. Danny E. Morris and Charles M. Olsen, *Discerning God's
Will Together: A Spiritual Practice for the Church* (Nashville: Upper
Room Books, 1997).

11. Richard Sennett, *The Fall of Public Man* (New York: Knopf,
1977), iv.